Fragile Rights

A Play

Frederick Bobor James

Sierra Leonean Writers Series

Fragile Rights

Copyright © 2017 by Frederick Bobor James
All rights reserved.

This is a work of fiction. Except in a few obvious instances, names, places, institutions and incidents are either products of the author's imagination or have been used fictitiously. Any resemblance to actual events, places, or persons alive or dead is purely coincidental

No part of this book may be reproduced in any form or by any electronic or mechanical means except by reviewers for the public press without written permission from the publishers.

ISBN: 978-99888-69-72-4

Sierra Leonean Writers Series

For downtrodden women
Who more often than not are
Excluded from programmes
Designed for their own freedom

Rights
Like biscuit
Break
Where least expected

FBJ

Fragile Rights/Frederick Bobor James

CHARACTERS

NJABU	Wife of Tom Kortuma, age 35 years.
ABIE BELIA	Friend of Njabu Kortuma and Chairwoman of the Women's Liberation Movement (WLM). Age 37 years.
TOM KORTUMA	Husband of Njabu, age 38 years.
BAINDU	First daughter of Tom and Njabu, age 12 years.
FENGEH	Second daughter of Tom and Njabu, age 10 years.
KOIVA	A client of the insurance company for which Njabu works.
MBETU	General Secretary of WLM.
PORSEH	Member of WLM.
FEREMUSU	Member of WLM.
YEALI	Member of WLM.
DAISY	Member of WLM.
FASIA	Boyfriend of Abie Belia.

Fragile Rights/Frederick Bobor James

NYANDA	Distant relation of Njabu and wife of Jumui.
JIMUI	Husband of Nyanda.
GBESSAY	Maid of Tom and Njabu and daughter of Jimui and Nyanda.
GHOST	Ghost of Gbessay's grandmother.
DOCTOR	Medical doctor.
NURSE	Hospital nurse.

GLOSSARY A glossary of local words used in the play is attached at the end.

Fragile Rights/Frederick Bobor James

ACT ONE, Scene One.

The forecourt of the National Insurance Company (NIC). Njabu Kortuma, age 35 years, works at the NIC. It is the end of the workday and she is rushing to beat the traffic. As she approaches her car, a former female college mate comes running to meet her.

Abie (*Smiling broadly, she embraces Njabu.*) Oh my God, is this Njabu, or my eyes are deceiving me? My dear sister I have caught up with you at long last.

Njabu Oh, my dear Abie. It has been such a long time. We last met at our convocation ceremony? You have become so famous. I listen to and watch your lectures on radio and television.

Abie (*They separate from their embrace.*) That's what brought me running over to meet you. The Women's Liberation Movement (WLM) needs brilliant women like you.

Njabu (*Smiles sheepishly.*) Brilliant, me brilliant?

Abie Njabu, you were so brilliant at university, and outspoken. We are all surprised that you dropped out of sight after graduation.

Fragile Rights/Frederick Bobor James

	By the way, how is life treating you?
Njabu	Oh, very well. Life is extremely kind to me.
Abie	What does that mean?
Njabu	A good husband, two lovely daughters and a good job.
Abie	And you are now rushing home to your luxury after work?
Njabu	Yes, my husband has to eat when he comes home from work.
Abie	Now wait a minute! You mean you are goig to cook after nine long hours at the office?
Njabu	I'm going to collect the children from a neighbour's house, take them home and cook for the family.
Abie	With such slavery, you say life is extremely kind to you?
Njabu	I enjoy it, Abie. A husband should eat meals prepared by his wife.
Abie	Does he insist on that?
Njabu	No, but that was one of the secrets to a

Fragile Rights/Frederick Bobor James

                happy marriage that my mother told me. "Your husband's feeding should be one of your primary concerns."

Abie   How about your freedom, and the freedom of womankind? A lot has gone wrong with you, Njabu. Let's have a meeting soon. Please give me your card.*(They exchange cards.)*

Light Fades.

Fragile Rights/Frederick Bobor James

ACT ONE, Scene Two.

The home of the Kortuma family. Njabu and family are sitting around the dining table eating.

Tom (*After the first mouthful.*) Hm, Njabu. This is altogether something different. Okra leaves and okra fruits combined in one sauce? The education you got from your mother and the *Sande* society put you above all women.

Njabu (*Beams with satisfaction.*) Tom, you always sound so native. With all your Western education! Or do you look beyond female genital mutilation (FGM) and see something good in *Sande*?

Tom But *Sande* is not all about FGM, is it?

Njabu There are now changing opinions about *Sande,* because it does FGM. But talking about it now will only spoil our appetite, please let us enjoy the food.

Baindu Dad, tomorrow I will cook the meal. Cassava leaves and broad beans. It will taste better than what Mum has done today.

Fengeh Dad, if Baindu cooks I will not eat the food.

Fragile Rights/Frederick Bobor James

	She does not know how to cook. (*About to cry.*)
Njabu	My darlings, I am patiently waiting for the time when you can go to the kitchen and cook very well for the family.
Fengeh	Then we will begin to compete with you for the kitchen. Dad will only eat food cooked by the one who knows best.
Njabu	When that time comes, we shall cook in turns. Not the best cook dominates the kitchen.
Tom	(*The family move to leave the dining room.*) My queens, tonight is storytime. Whose turn is it to tell a story?
Baindu	Dad, it is your turn.
Tom	Well, fetch the mat in your room. (*The children dash for the mat.*) Who knows, one of them may grow up to become a storyteller. Knowing our folktales and fables will help with their education. We must not allow our oral literature to die. If we do, it will be a disaster. (*Tom and the girls are now seated on the mat in a semi-circle. Njabu is in the kitchen.*) One day, Spider went to help his in-laws on the farm.

Fragile Rights/Frederick Bobor James

Fengeh   Oh Dad! Spider again?

Tom   Yes, Spider. You have a lot yet to learn about this man.

Baindu   But Dad, is Spider really a man?

Tom   He was a real man before he turned into an insect.

Baindu   Dad, did you see him before he turned into a spider?

Tom   That was a long time ago.

Baindu   But who told you all these stories about Spider?

Tom   Keima, my grandmother.

Fengeh   You are asking too many questions, Baindu. Dad, please go on.

Tom   Before Spider set out for the farm in the morning, his mother-in-law roasted twelve cups of groundnuts for him to eat on his way.

Fengeh   Dad, that man was a glutton. Twelve cups of groundnuts?

Fragile Rights/Frederick Bobor James

Baindu:	Dad, I hope you are not lying! (*They all laugh in chorus.*)
Tom	If it is a lie, then it is a lie when Goat and Elephant had an eating contest. (*Njabu appears from the kitchen.*)
Njabu	The children have to go to bed, Tom.
Baindu	Mum, please let us hear this story.
Fengeh	Yes, Mum, please!
Tom	One day Elephant and Goat challenged each other to an eating contest. Goat said that he could eat more than Elephant. Elephant said the goat's mouth was too small to produce such words.
Baindu	Dad, how can an animal as small as a goat go against an elephant? I cannot imagine how these two animals could compete for anything.
Fengeh	But wait, Baindu. Don't you think this could be another David and Goliath story?
Baindu	Please Dad, let us hear the rest of the story.
Tom	The contest was set up and the next day, Goat and Elephant went to the field to

Fragile Rights/Frederick Bobor James

	graze.
Baindu	Were they given the same food?
Tom	Because they both do not eat the same food stuff, the rule was to graze from sunrise to sunset. And there were people hired to watch them eat.
Fengeh	Was that a fair contest, Dad?
Baindu	But Goliath had all the armour. Was it fair that he had to fight an unarmed boy like David?
Tom	They both ate the whole day and at sunset went and rested on the high rocks that were around.
Baindu	But how were the organisers able to know who had eaten more than the other?
Tom	As they both rested on the rocks, tired and sleepy, Goat began to chew his gum. "What are you doing?" Elephant asked Goat. "Eating rocks," replied Goat. "And when I finish, I will eat you next." Elephant ran away, and that is why he is afraid of Goat even today. *(The children burst into laughter.)*

Light Fades.

Fragile Rights/Frederick Bobor James

ACT ONE, Scene Three.

Home of Abie Belia. It is midnight of the same day she bumped into Njabu. She returns to an empty house and goes straight for a bath.

Abie (*The WLM song plays on a stereo as she bathes.*)

Chorus
On female shoulders
Ride males to the top,
Once at the top they
Turn their willing ladders into serfs,
To nurse their egos.

Song
From their ribs we came
But in our wombs we carry them,
Suckle them on our breasts
And watch over their feeble steps.

As children and adults
We play matching roles,
If we respect and accept each other's strength,
Together we overcome obstacles.

Let us in the classrooms sit in equal numbers,
Learn mathematics, engineering,

Fragile Rights/Frederick Bobor James

the sciences and medicine together,
Qualify in equal numbers
And share jobs more equally.

Let us together run the state,
Women not as passive observers
But side by side with their menfolk,
To carve the welfare of our children.

Let us plan the sizes of our families together
Run the homes and rear our children in harmony,
Women not just as incubators and breeders,
Forever on their knees welcoming home
Their husbands from work adorned in coat and tie.

From your ribs we were created
But in our wombs we carry you,
Suckle and anoint you day and night
And watch over your weak steps.

Climb down from our shoulders;
Let's walk and work as equals
For a better world for our children
And ourselves.

(She returns to the parlour and is eating take-away food she has brought home. She stops eating abruptly. Mocking Njabu's voice.) My husband

should eat a meal prepared by his wife. My mother told me, "Your husband's feeding should be one of your primary concerns." Why did she remind me of these backward-looking words? My mother rang them in my ears again and again. So did every illiterate woman whose daughter was in higher education.*(Pause.)* I don't have the joy of coming home to a family after work. But I'm happy I am doing it for the freedom of womankind. Including Njabu, whose university education has enslaved rather than free her. *(Pacing.)* How long shall we sit down and watch all these ills going on against women? *(The song "On female shoulders, Ride males to the top" begins to filter in softly as she sits down to eat. Rises to go to bed after eating.)*

Light Fades.

Fragile Rights/Frederick Bobor James

ACT ONE, Scene Four.

NJABU'S OFFICE.

Njabu (*Telephone rings and she takes the call.*)
Hello, Njabu here!

Abie Hi! It's me, your sister, Abie.

Njabu Abie, my dear, how was your night?

Abie Oh, it was fantastic, and yours?

Njabu It could not have been better.

Abie My darling Njabu, after we talked yesterday, I could not stop thinking that it's time you joined the women's movement, the Women's Liberation Movement (WLM).

Njabu Come on Abie, I am too busy to join any movement or organisation.

Abie Your problem is that you have been tamed by that lame husband of yours.

Njabu (*Frowns.*) What makes a good wife?

Fragile Rights/Frederick Bobor James

Abie (*Chuckles.*) What's your assessment of a good husband?

Njabu I want yours first.

Abie *Chuckles again.*) A lame duck of course. Only a stupid woman looks for a fast and loose man for a husband.

Njabu What in hell's name do you mean?

Abie The broken hearted, ask the broken hearted. (*Pause.*)

Njabu Hello, Abie, are you there?

Abie By the way, how about joining us in the Atlantic Hall of the National Stadium at 7:00 pm today?

Njabu Oh, dear! How will my family fit into this? You know it is impossible, Abie.

Abie Njabu please, you must know you have a role to play in this revolution.

Njabu Revolution?

Abie We are not talking guns, but the liberation of our women.

Fragile Rights/Frederick Bobor James

Njabu Liberate the women?

Abie Njabu, please do not tell me they are not in chains. Their plight is surely more serious than people in jail.

Njabu Abie, I need more time to think about all this. I cannot attend today. (*Pause.*) Abie, Abie can you hear me?

Abie I can hear you, Njabu. Look, I don't care if you come one hour late. But do come. You can stay for 15, 30 minutes and then leave. Please come.

Njabu Abie, I will try. But I will not give you an answer now. If you see me, you see me. If you don't, you don't. (*As the telephone conversation ends, Njabu looks at the ceiling in confusion.*)

Koiva (*Koiva who has been standing at the door eavesdropping on the telephone conversation, walks in quietly. Njabu is startled to see him.*) Madam, I didn't mean to scare you.

Njabu (*Both hands are pressed on her chest in skock.*) Please forgive me for being terrified by your presence. Please take a seat.

Fragile Rights/Frederick Bobor James

Koiva (*Takes a seat facing Njabu.*) Thank you very much, Madam.

Njabu How can I help you?

Koiva Madam, I want to start a transport company with buses plying the routes to Kenema, Bo, Makeni, and shuttling from Freetown to its outskirts and back. I want your company to handle the insurance for the whole fleet.

Njabu (*Sits up.*) Great news! We shall be delighted to do business with you. How many vehicles are we talking about?

Koiva Twenty-four to start with.

Njabu Please let me give you our policy documents to read. When you are ready, do come back. (*Hands him the documents.*)

Koiva (*Rises to go.*) Please expect me soon. (*Exits.*)

Njabu (*She tidies her desk to leave the office.*) I have not even joined this movement yet and I have already started keeping customers waiting. However, I will go and see what it looks like. It probably is one of those gossipy women's groups. (*She exits.*)

Fragile Rights/Frederick Bobor James

Light Fades.
ACT TWO, Scene One.

Home of the Kortumas.

Baindu	*(Njabu and children eating.)* Mummy, we are home early today and you have already cooked.
Njabu	Yes darling, I am rushing to attend a meeting.
Fengeh	Mummy, what type of meeting?
Njabu	A meeting of a women's liberation group.
Baindu	You mean the meeting will be only for women?
Njabu	That was what I was told.
Baindu	Is there a group for men, too?
Njabu	Oh, the men are already liberated. They don't need a group for that.
Baindu	How about the children, are they liberated, too?
Njabu	Children and women belong to the group of people known as the voiceless and

Fragile Rights/Frederick Bobor James

Fengeh	vulnerable. But Mummy, I do not understand what you mean by voiceless and vulnerable.
Njabu	I mean those who are not listened to in making decisions, and those who are weak or exposed to all the ills.(*Njabu and the children finish eating. She puts the dishes away, switches on the television, and kisses them goodbye.*)
Baindu	(*Njabu is about to step out.*) Mum, are you not going to wait for Dad to come before you leave?
Njabu	I will be late for the meeting.
Bainu	Mum, you've never left us alone in this house before. Daddy will be very angry if he meets us all alone in this big house.
Njabu	Don't worry, your Dad will understand (*She leaves.*)

The Light Goes Out.

Fragile Rights/Frederick Bobor James

ACT TWO, Scene Two.

Njabu attends the WLM meeting for the first time.

Abie (*Njabu arrives as the meeting is about to start.*) Ladies, let us please rise and welcome our sister by singing our solidarity song "*On female shoulders, Ride males to the top.*" (*The women rise and sing in a jubilant mood.*)

Chorus
On female shoulders
Ride males to the top,
And at the top
Turn their willing ladders into serfs,
To nurse their egos. (They sing the song to the end.)

Please let us sit down. Before I address this meeting, I want to introduce the new arrival. She is Njabu Kortuma (Mrs.). Someone we have longed to bring on board. She has an honours degree in Accounting, with a string of diplomas in Insurance. Very well employed. She is indeed a big catch. We need to congratulate ourselves. (*They sing the chorus of the solidarity song again and she starts the address.*) At this meeting, we are going to discuss the gender issues we want to address in the next three

Fragile Rights/Frederick Bobor James

Mbetu	years. These are the same issues we will talk about at the Regional Conference in three weeks time. I will stop here and ask the WLM General Secretary to read them to us.
Mbetu	(*The Secretary General raises her fist.*) Power to the women!
Chorus	Enormous power!
Mbetu	I have the honour to read to you this evening the five gender issues that WLM proposes to address in the next three years. They are: 1) Violence against women; 2) Right of women to formal education; 3) Equal job opportunities, 4) Right of women to take part in decision making at domestic, local and central government levels; 5) and finally, the right of women to keep their maiden names after marriage.
Abie	Let us give our dynamic General Secretary a big hand. (*Thunderous applause.*) We have all heard the five items read by the General Secretary. The floor is now open for questions and comments. (*A hand goes up.*) I will take the first question from this row. Please make sure you are very brief. Yes, Porseh.
Porseh	May I please know how you came by these

Fragile Rights/Frederick Bobor James

five issues? As far as I am concerned, the most important is women doing all the housework whilst the men enjoy, and on top of that beat their partners.

Abie The five issues were agreed upon by a committee put together by all of us. This is debatable, however. Yes, I can see another hand, Madam Feremusu.

Feremusu The issue of women being seen only as breeders needs serious consideration. (*Rejoinders from one or two.*)

Yeali I agree with you, my sister, particularly when the costs of raising a child keep going up. Consider the high cost of education alone!

Daisy Most of our men are worthless. Once they have got a woman pregnant, they do not care what happens to the baby and the mother.

Abie: I can see that there are many important issues relating to gender inequality that need to be addressed. But you can all agree with me that we cannot handle all of them at once. The next time we meet we shall select our representatives to the Regional Conference.

Fragile Rights/Frederick Bobor James

Daisy I think what is needed now is to approve and adopt these five issues, so that they become a working document for WLM over the next three years. And to present them at the up-coming Regional Conference.

Abie You are right, Daisy. I now ask your permission for the General Secretary to table the issues for your approval. GS, please.

Mbetu I will read the issues one by one. After I have read each one, you will approve it by show of hands. (*A hand goes up.*) Yes, Yeali.

Yeali What if an issue does not receive the majority vote from this body?

Abie We shall put it aside for further discussion, or replacement. Does that please everyone?

Chorus Ye-ees. (*The GS goes through the list and all the items are carried.*)

Abie I am sure we are all happy that in three years we shall be addressing the problems that affect our womenfolk the most.

Fragile Rights/Frederick Bobor James

Chorus Ye-ees. (*They burst into the chorus of their solidarity song.*)

Abie At this point, I want to ask for the adjournment of this meeting, can someone move it?

Chorus We mo-oo-vee!

Abie: Because the Regional Conference is coming soon, the meeting is adjourned for two days.

The Light Goes Out.

Fragile Rights/Frederick Bobor James

ACT TWO, Scene Three.

At the Kortumas, Tom finds the children alone at home.

Tom (*Fengeh is sleeping in the chair.*) Come on, what's going on here? My darling sleeping in the chair? (*He takes Fengeh in his arms and kisses her.*) Where is Mummy?

Baindu She has gone to a meeting of women.

Tom She what?

Fengeh Went to a meeting.

Tom Have you both eaten?

Chorus Yes.

Tom You say your mother went out and left just the two of you in this big house?

Baindu Dad, she said you would understand.

Tom Understand what?

Fengeh Why she has gone to this meeting.

Tom When she gets home, I will give her a stern

	warning. I don't think this will be good for the security of my children. All girls, as a matter of fact!
Njabu	(*As Njabu enters, she goes straight over to Tom and hugs him, but he gives her a cold shoulder.*) My dear Tom, have you been back for long?
Tom	Just a little while ago, but where is this new behaviour coming from?
Njabu	(*Looks lost for words.*) Well Tom, I, I needed to go to a women's meeting this evening.
Tom	(*Smiles weakly.*) I hope this is not going to continue. If the children were old enough, I would have no objection.
Njabu	(*Smiling.*) But wait a minute, Tom. Is there anything wrong with us sharing the care of the children after work?
Tom	For example?
Njabu	If I have to come home late, you collect the children and bring them home.
Tom	And maybe prepare food for the home, and take the children through their homework and revise their lessons with them?

Fragile Rights/Frederick Bobor James

Njabu   If there is need Tom, why not?

Tom   Ehm, and what else?

Njabu   Tom, won't it be fun to go to the kitchen with your darling daughters and cook a meal when their Mum is away?

Tom   These new ideas of yours make my head spin. We need to go to bed now. The children rise early for school tomorrow. *(The children go to their room and Tom and Njabu to theirs.)*

Light Goes Out.

Fragile Rights/Frederick Bobor James

ACT TWO, Scene Four.

It is early in the morning. The Kortuma family is preparing for work and school.

Njabu (*Calls out to Tom who is in the bedroom.*) Tom, I am going to see that the children wash and dress for school. Please boil some water for tea.

Tom (*Rushes into the parlour, shaking with rage.*) What did my ears hear?

Njabu (*Stammers the words.*) I said, please help me with one of the chores this morning. Boil water for tea, while I help the children to wash and dress.

Tom (*Trying to control his anger.*) And then do what? Wash the dishes, prepare breakfast and then set the table for Njabu and the kids to eat, eh? With Tom waiting on them, eh?

Njabu But I have asked you to help me with only one task.

Tom I can see the other tasks written on your forehead. You are only waiting for me to start doing the first one.

Fragile Rights/Frederick Bobor James

Njabu	Who was cooking your meals, cleaning your room, and washing your dirty linens when you were studying abroad?
Tom	You know the typical African male does chores only when there is no one to do them for him.
Njabu	And so?
Tom	Tom will not go to the kitchen this morning. He goes to the kitchen only out of pleasure, not at any one's behest.
Njabu	And Njabu?
Tom	Oh, out of duty, and Njabu knows that very well. That has been the practice here, I don't know where these strange new ideas are coming from.
Chorus	Dad and Mum, we are running late!
Tom	My queens, I don't think your mother should go to this women's meeting any more. I can already see trouble brewing for this home.
Fengeh	Mum, from now on, you should be going to men's meetings.

Fragile Rights/Frederick Bobor James

Tom	As a matter of fact, she must not attend a meeting of any sort. Let us hurry up, we have only thirty minutes left. *(They go to their rooms to prepare for school and work.)*

Light Goes Out.

Fragile Rights/Frederick Bobor James

ACT TWO, Scene Five.

NJABU'S OFFICE.

Njabu	(*The telephone rings.*) Hello, Njabu speaking. Who am I talking to?
Abie	Oh, come on, you should know my voice by now. You are talking to Abie.
Njabu	Aah, Abie!
Abie	How did you enjoy the meeting yesterday?
Njabu	That meting as well as the movement are a revelation and revolution.
Abie	What do you mean?
Njabu	It caused a lot of problems between my husband and me yesterday evening, as well as this morning.
Abie	I don't understand. You mean…?
Njabu	Tom came out clearly this morning that he is not made to do chores around the house.
Abie	He cannot share housework with you?

Fragile Rights/Frederick Bobor James

Njabu	He was shaking with anger this morning when I asked him to boil water for tea, while I washed and dressed the children for school.
Abie	Ideally, you should have asked him to do the reverse.
Njabu	I agree with you, but the children are both girls. One bears the name of his mother, and the other the name of his grandmother. He does not even call them by their names, let alone bathe, and dress them.
Abie	If you stand up to him two or more times on this, he will give in. They are a bunch of cowards.
Njabu	(*Laughs.*) I think we have to go slowly with this revolution. After all, the men are our husbands and the fathers of our children.
Abie	Gradually? And the men overwork us, rape and deny us our rights? Come on Njabu, you shouldn't take a soft stance on the antics of men.
Njabu	Actually, this is the only time we have quarrelled in front of the children in all the thirteen years we have been together as husband and wife.

Fragile Rights/Frederick Bobor James

Abie   First quarrels always bring violent reactions from men. You are lucky you did not get a few hot slaps.

Njabu   I am sure I was saved by the presence of the children, and their pleading eyes.

Abie   Men fear opposition, you know. Do it as often as it is necessary. You will soon be allowed to contribute to decisions at home. Your voice will be heard. And you will get him to go to the kitchen one fine day.

Njabu   (*In deep thought.*) I will try. Bye for now. (*Stares at the ceiling as if in a daze.*) This is a difficult decision to make. The visibility and dignity of womankind, at the expense of the peace and unity of my home. (*Walking away from her seat.*) But only yesterday I was given a heroine's welcome by these very women. How can I desert them now. I will go along with them as far as I can.

Light fades as Njabu takes her seat.

Fragile Rights/Frederick Bobor James

ACT TWO, Scene Six.

Home of Abie.

Abie (*Expecting a visitor, as she prepares food.*)
He tells me "I run away from a bossy wife into the arms of an even bossier woman. I think I should have little or nothing to do with women." I wonder what I can do to make him stay. Carry him on my back, rock him and sing a lullaby for him? (*Mimicking*).

Stop, stop, Fasia, stop crying
Today your mother went fishing
In the great whirlpool
And will in the evening bring for you
A hamper full of giant crayfish and crabs
And you will eat until your stomach
Reaches bursting point
Stop, stop, Fasia, stop crying.

(*Laughs*). Men, like children, love to be pampered. They are babies in adult skin. (*Doorbell rings and Abie goes to see who it is.*)

Fasia It is me, Fasia.

Abie (*They hug as the door opens.*) Please come in. You look tipsy, Fas.

Fragile Rights/Frederick Bobor James

Fasia	I have to be. That woman is driving me crazy.
Abie	Men don't ever drive women crazy, do they?
Fasia	You know women drive men crazy more often than men do women. It is even more rampant now, with this new movement manned by…
Abie	It is a women's movement headed by a woman, it is not manned.
Fasia	(Laughs half-heartedly.) Ah, you mean womanned by…
Abie	No teasing. You are running away from a leopard, do not start calling for a lion.
Fasia	Something terrible has gone wrong with our generation.
Abie	(*Both now at table.*) What is wrong with our generation?
Fasia	Some of the traditional female chores have been assigned to men. I now do the dishes, clean the toilet, wash my own clothes…
Abie	I do not see anything wrong with that,

	especially if your wife works long office hours like you.
Fasia	You cannot, because it does not matter to you if men doing women's work hurts men's pride or not.
Abie	(*Abie looks at him and smiles.*) You must stop defending men's egos at the expense of the rights of the women. They are human beings like the men, and they have rights like them.

Light Goes Out.

Fragile Rights/Frederick Bobor James

ACT THREE, Scene One.

Home of the Kortumas. The time is 11:00pm.

Njabu (*Njabu runs to the living room, followed by Tom.*) Tom, Tom, you know night is meant for people to sleep off their day's stress. But you don't allow me to sleep at all at night! Why are you so headstrong?

Tom But why do you ask such a question? Tom or Njabu, who is getting more stubborn every day?

Njabu (*Keeping a distance from Tom.*) It is Njabu who disturbs day and night, and doesn't allow Tom time to sleep at night.

Tom You mean Njabu bothers Tom when he is pretending to be sleeping?

Njabu: What I know is that Njabu does not disturb Tom at night when he is sleeping. If only Tom could do the same.

Tom: (*Walking away.*) Tom is a wild animal from the jungle. How can he behave better? Maybe with training from his mistress, he can change his behaviour.

Fragile Rights/Frederick Bobor James

Njabu (*Laughing mischievously.*) I could have had some sleep by now if my Tom were not a nightime nuisance.

Tom: The fact is that my Njabu is having her way far too much now. She brings bedroom secrets into the open and makes Tom look silly.

Njabu Bedroom games need consent from both players. Otherwise, one will be infringing on the right and dignity of the other and will be guilty of abuse or violation.

Tom: I violate my own wife now? What a bizarre thought learnt from a feminist movement! (*They both move into their bedroom clumsily.*)

Light Goes Out.

Fragile Rights/Frederick Bobor James

ACT THREE, Scene Two.

The following morning at the home of the Kortumas. The family is about to leave for work.

Njabu I am attending a WLM meeting this afternoon, Tom. Please collect the children from the neighbour's and do prepare food for the family when you bring them home.

Tom (*Looks enraged.*) I hate to quarrel in the morning. I hate to…

Njabu Come on, Tom, you should try and understand.

Tom We have to make an alternative arrangement, Njabu. We cannot go on like this.

Njabu We should make sure the children are in school on time. That is more important to me this morning than quarrelling.

Tom (*Going towards the bedroom.*) Njabu is the most reasonable person in this house now. Tom is the quarrel monger.

Njabu Girls, let's go. We have to be off before the traffic gets heavy. (*The girls run on stage ready for school.*)
 Light goes off.

Fragile Rights/Frederick Bobor James

ACT THREE, Scene Three.

Home of Abie. Fasia is about to leave after a night's visit.

Fasia	I think I should come back tomorrow evening and spend the weekend here.
Abie	You have to make up your mind, darling.
Fasia	I feel so secure here that I do not want to go home again.
Abie	No, you cannot afford to stay here forever. You have a home to go to.
Fasia	And a home to run to when I feel threatened.
Abie	(*Angry.*) Oh no, don't come here any more!
Fasia	(*By her side.*) Honey, if you stop me from coming here, where will I run to?
Abie	Like all men, you only care about your own happiness. That is all. By the way, Fasia, are you going home before you go to work?
Fasia:	What is your concern?

Fragile Rights/Frederick Bobor James

Abie: I wonder what excuse you will give for…

Fasia: You should have said something earlier.

Abie Fas, you sound paranoid!

Fasia I do?

Abie It shows in the way you do everything.

Fasia With you women on the warpath, many men are going to live in paranoia. The men are going to live in hell. (*Walks to the door.*)

Abie (*Rushes after him.*) Listen to me, we are not waging war. We are asking for what is due us. We want to be regarded as equal partners. That is all.

Fasia You want to reverse the roles prescribed for us by God.

Abie Roles! You mean men as loafers, holding the womenfolk in serfdom?

Fasia Women as serfs?

Abie Yes, from genesis we have been your slaves. We bear and rear your children and babysit you, too. What do women have to show for all this drudgery?

Fasia (*Looking helpless.*) Oh, and I thought I was secure here. You now suggest I have jumped from the frying pot to the fire?

Abie (*Sobbing softly.*) We have to continue this struggle. It does not matter what, and we are bent to win it.

Light Fades Out.

Fragile Rights/Frederick Bobor James

ACT THREE, Scene Four.

Njabu's Office.

Njabu (*Pacing the room.*) Tom complains of being pushed too far. He is refusing to accept change. I now begin to understand Mama's rule more clearly. If a woman wants to be happily married, she has to be a slave to her husband. Go to the kitchen, prepare his meal, stay home and look after his children, and babysit him, too. (*A client is waiting to be ushered in.*) I have been going by my mother's recipe for a successful marriage for a while now. Now I realize that her recipe is not for our generation. The times have changed. Tom and I both go to work in the morning and come home tired in the evening. Yet, he expects me to do all the chores alone. (*Pauses, turns round and sees the client waiting to be ushered in.*) Oh no, I am sorry my dear.

Koiva (*Smiles broadly.*) Never mind, Madam.

Njabu You should have let me know you are around. You mean you heard all these …? Oh my God!

Koiva Madam, I am sorry for intruding. As a matter of fact, the probem of gender

	equality is quite common nowadays. (*Smiles pleasantly.*) We men are too lazy, leaving wives to do all the housework. It is even worse for women whose husbands are farmers.
Njabu	The truth of the matter is that some of you African men don't want to change; including the so-called Western educated. You want to live like your great, great-grandparents. In spite of the technological advancement.
Koiva	Gender equality is a new phenomenon. We have to learn how to live with it, both men and women. It has come to stay.
Njabu	(*Smiles dryly.*) Sorry to bother you with a domestic matter.
Koiva	Never mind. The rights of women is universal.
Njabu	How do you find our policy?
Koiva:	Wonderful. That is why I have come back.
Njabu:	(*Handing him forms.*) Please fill out these forms, and we will start doing business right away. (*Koiva filling in the forms.*) *Light Geos Out.*

Fragile Rights/Frederick Bobor James

ACT THREE, Scene Five.

Women's Liberation Movement Meeting.

Abie (*After their women's liberation song.*)
Thank you, my sisters, for keeping the fire burning. I know gender equality is catching on everywhere in this country. We are making in-roads. We have broken the glass ceiling in engineering, accounting, you name it. We have arrived! We are in Parliament and Cabinet. Give us five years and we will capture the Vice Presidency and from there walk straight to the Presidency.

Chorus Forward with WLM! Backward never!

Abie: Now, to the agenda for this meeting. WLM representation at the Regional Conference on Gender in Dakar, Senegal. Five people have been selected. They include the Chairwoman, the General Secretary, the Organizing Secretary, the Financial Secretary and our sister, Mrs. Njabu Kortuma, a co-opted member of the executive. (*Some members frown at the mention of Njabu's name.*) The conference is nearly three weeks away. The representatives have enough time to plan and get permission from their husbands and employers. I see a hand up.

Fragile Rights/Frederick Bobor James

Yes?

Daisy It looks like this movement is becoming top-heavy. I do not hate our sister, Njabu, but I hate the way she has been selected to attend this international conference. When did she join the movement?

Yeali Yesterday, the day before yesterday, today, or tomorrow? I cannot remember.

Mbetu We have mountains to climb. We should not be stopped by small barriers put in our way by kids playing in the sand.

Daisy We must take our cues from those small barriers. We are too busy with the big things, leaving undone those little things that will later undo us as a movement.

Abie You are trying to distract us, Daisy. This kind of talk is uncalled for. You should allow the meeting to go on as planned.

Yeali Is this not supposed to be a forum where every member has the right to express her views? Is the WLM now the personal property of the executive and degree holders?

Abie How can you say that, Yeali?

Fragile Rights/Frederick Bobor James

Yeali But if we begin to discriminate against ourselves, we who are at the core of the movement here in the city, then what's at stake for women in the villages?

Daisy Do we have on the delegation a representative from the grassroots in the provinces, or even here in Freetown?

Abie Why are you raising such issues only now?

Daisy Because we think, talk, and travel for our vulnerable women. Whose rights are we promoting? Our own rights, our own voices, and our own image? What if people accuse us of being self promoters?

Yeali Daisy is right, this movement is not about ourselves, but the common woman.

Abie Daisy and Yeali, you are trying to tear this movement apart. Some of us are making great sacrifices for this movement.

Yeali We all are. What we are trying to say is that, we should not be seen to be promoting only our own interests. Rights, yes, but whose rights? We need to define that more carefully. We are supposed to help speed up change in this whole process. If we don't, we will be accused of mere lip service.

Fragile Rights/Frederick Bobor James

Daisy	When the Regional Conference is over, our job should be the three-year programme. Develop a plan that will make more people we are fighting for take part in the movement fully.
Yeali	And benefit from the movement. After all, it is their movement.
Njabu	There is much wisdom in what Daisy and Yeali are saying. We need to build this movement on solid ground. Our people say that if one is accused of being a witch, her mouth should always be fastened upon the wall.
Abie	Eating the mud or brick wall until you get your mouth at the occupants. That is the spirit!
Njabu	One grassroots member should travel on my own ticket.
Mbetu	There is no such member in our register.
Abie	Even if we have a grassroots member, you should not walk out of this trip. It will cast doubt on the movement.
Daisy	We can now see that we have a good reason for changing this movement.

Fragile Rights/Frederick Bobor James

Mbetu	Can we now continue with the discussion on the conference?
Yeali	Yes, we can. Our people say that when your relative or friend is head of a secret society, you cannot be deprived of the juiciest part of the ritual meal.
Porseh	Five representatives from WLM. Who sponsors them?
Abie	Two international non-governmental organisations (NGOs) working in gender and children's rights have said they will provide airline tickets and daily subsistence allowances (DSA) for each delegate.
Feremusu	How about letters of invitation for us to show our bosses and husbands?
Abie	Thank you for reminding me. The letters of invitation, tickets, as well as DSAs will be issued tomorrow to facilitate our travel arrangements.
Mbetu	Where do we get the tickets, the other documents and DSAs from?
Abie	Please collect them from my office tomorrow between 2:00pm and 7:00pm. I now want to declare this meeting over.

Fragile Rights/Frederick Bobor James

Daisy Before we leave, I warn that we think about the way forward. We have to let the men know that we are not at war with them. We have to coax them. Our people say that when you want to dress a very tall mask devil, you should do so when it is lying down.

Abie Daisy, a severe illness requires a severe treatment. That is what our people say, also. We have to be forceful, and make sacrifices. We have to let the men know that we mean business.

Daisy I think we have to adopt the wisdom in the old parable: kill the ant carefully so you can see its guts. That certainly requires a lot of patience.

Abie But we are killing no ant. We are trying to cut up a giant. We have to use the right instruments. Please, Daisy, let us not be cowards.

Daisy My philosophy is that we should not fight this battle by throwing our weapons at the enemies. If we do, they will use them to run after us. It is our children who will suffer in the end. Our people say that a mother hen must not jump over fire.

Fragile Rights/Frederick Bobor James

Abie Please let us leave now. We can hold an executive meeting to look at our approach some more.

As members depart, light goes out.

Fragile Rights/Frederick Bobor James

ACT THREE, Scene Six.

Scene switches to the home of the Kortuma family. Tom is telling stories to the kids.

Tom (*Seated with the kids on a mat.*) This time Spider went to weave for his in-laws.

Fengeh Daddy, Spider again?

Tom Yes, Spider. The more you know about Spider the more you will know about mankind.

Fengeh Daddy, I cannot see the link.

Tom You will find the link in time. Spider had begun weaving. His mother-in-law, who was boiling cassava for him to eat, went to the stream to fetch water.

Baindu Didn't they have water in the house already?

Tom Maybe they did not have enough.

Fengeh Was he as greedy as the last Spider?

Tom We will soon know if this one too is a glutton or not.

Fragile Rights/Frederick Bobor James

Baindu Please Dad, continue. I want to know if all Spiders behave in the same greedy way.

Tom Spider could not wait for his mother-in-law to come back from the stream and dish up the cassava.

Fengeh What did he do, then?

Tom He took one chunk from the pot. Soon, he saw his mother-in-law returning from the stream. He put the hot cassava on his head, covered it with his cap, and began to sing and weave.

Song
When grandma goes to fetch water
She comes running back
Before you can even wink your eyes (*Repeat song several times. The children laugh in chorus. Whilst they are busy laughing, Njabu arrives.*)

Njabu (*Pats children gently on their backs and attempts to hug Tom.*) Oh, what a wonderful husband I have here.

Tom (*Moves away and mimics Njabu.*) Oh yes, my wife now has a willing servant. One that has taken over her housekeeping. Now from work she wanders around, comes back home after he has done her chores.

Fragile Rights/Frederick Bobor James

Njabu (*Amused.*) Tom, I want you to accept the fact that we both go to work in the morning and come back home tired. If we get home about the same time, we have to help each other cook, and then clean the kitchen. Whoever comes home first should go to the kitchen and do what is needed.

Tom (*Looks angry and paces wildly.*) You are now in charge of this home. You can rule it the way you want. If you tell me sit there, I will. You can even get a cane and whip me. Tom will lie flat on the floor for Njabu to flog him, then he will rise up and say, thank you, Madam.

Njabu My God, Tom, have you been drinking, or you are pretending to have lost your mind? (*Begins to weep softly.*) Why can't we have peace and unity in this house anymore? Why, Tom, why?

Baindu (*Both children put their arms around their mother and look up at her with concern.*) Mum, what has gone wrong this time?

Njabu There is something wrong with your Dad, which you are too young to understand. It is eating away at this family.

Fengeh There is nothing wrong with Dad. Just now

Fragile Rights/Frederick Bobor James

	he was telling us a story. We were laughing with him. Beside, he is very kind to us.
Baindu	Mummy, maybe you should stop going to this women's meeting after work. Dad loves you; he wants you to be around for us always.
Njabu	Fold your mats and go to bed. Your Dad's problem is much bigger than that. (*The children fold their mats and go to their bedroom, and Njabu goes to their own bedroom.*)
Tom	(*Alone in the parlour. Tom walks to the cupboard, pours himself a full glass of whisky and gulps half of it.*) I cannot lose control of this home. If I do, it will be a disaster for the children. (*Takes another gulp.*) You see, I love my Njabu and my daughters. I have known no other woman. From work, straight home to my Njabu and my daughters. Njabu has always done the same. Now that she has become too big for this house, taking orders from God knows who. I am losing control. (*Begins to pace.*) If it wasn't for my daughters, I would have walked out. But these poor angels, one is named after my mother, and the other after my grandmother. And Tom runs away and leaves them behind? For whom? Their mother who is slowly leaving us?

Fragile Rights/Frederick Bobor James

Njabu *(Joins Tom in the parlour.)* Tom darling, I will be attending a Gender Regional Conference out of Sierra Leone three weeks from today. I will be away for ten days.

Tom *(Shouting every sentence.)* That is a matter between you and your employers. I am just a servant in this home. You do not need approval from me to do anything anymore. But…!

Njabu *(Interrupts Tom.)* But, what?

Tom My children. I am worried about what all of this will do to my children. Your new attitude to this family is trouble for the future of my children.

Njabu *(Confused.)* Tom, I think I have a duty to give some of my time to the fight for women's freedom. We have to fight for a brighter future for our daughters and womenfolk. A future free of male domination, free of violence against women, and free of control.

Tom *(Angry.)* For God's sake, leave my children out of the foreign ideas of you and your followers. These ideas are going to affect them in a bad way. They will become misfits in their own country. Not to talk of

Fragile Rights/Frederick Bobor James

their villages!

Njabu We are looking past village and country, Tom. We want our women, and girls, to be as free as women and girls in the developed world.

Tom Aha, is that what you know? They may be seeing the light at the end of the tunnel, but they are not there yet.

Njabu If we get as far as they have, the likes of Tom will have been cooperating with their wives by now.

Tom Njabu, if this is the way your organisation is fighting for freedom for the women, I can see problems in many homes.

Njabu (*Walking away.*) I must go to the conference. I must. No matter how helpless you feel, Tom.

Tom You don't understand. Who said anything about stopping you from going? You should by now know what I feel about the meetings and the time they are taking away from our family life.

Njabu Tom, it is time we talked about this matter in a useful way. Sulking and getting angry

Fragile Rights/Frederick Bobor James

will not solve the problem.

Tom The problem is your making. You find a solution to it.

Njabu We may need a maid to look after the house and the children. Maybe that will help?

Tom I would be most pleased if you could look for one. Please do so before you leave us for your conference. *(Njabu walks back to the bedroom. Tom stays in the parlour alone, looking at the ceiling.)*

The Light Fades.

Fragile Rights/Frederick Bobor James

ACT THREE, Scene Seven.

Abie's House.

Abie (*Kneeling on the floor before Fasia.*) I drove you out the other day. That was rude of me, please stay as long as you can this time.

Fasia (*Stroking her hair.*) You know what? It is stupid for any man to look for traditional comforts in the company of a modern woman. I have begun to learn how to take commands from my wife. I mean living as equal partners.

Abie If only all modern African men could begin to think like you, there will be less tension in married homes.

Fasia I think this battle should be fought without violence; without making enemies, and even without separation and divorce.

Abie It seems like this is going to be a difficult fight. It has already started making us, the leaders, crazy.

Fasia The problem is that, you bite more than you can chew.

Fragile Rights/Frederick Bobor James

Abie	(*Apologetic.*) I know that you are starting something that would make you run out of this house again.
Fasia	(*Smiles in her face.*) Don't get upset now, I am going to learn how to live with you, too.
Abie	That is the best thing to say now. It is learning to live with the tigress and not taming her.
Fasia	But both words are nearly the same.
Abie	Yes, but one word says taming, while the other says working together.

Light Fades.

Fragile Rights/Frederick Bobor James

ACT THREE, Scene Eight.

At the home of Jimui and his wife, a distant relation of Njabu. Both husband and wife are above fifty years of age.

Nyanda   My dear Jimui, I had a strange dream last night. One that I have never had in all my life.

Jimui   And you kept quiet about it the whole day. Now you have lost the chance to stop its power through a sacrifice to the gods. What if it is an ill omen designed to reach us in half a day?

Nyanda   The dream walked out of my memory and never came back until now.

Jimui   Nyanda, such forgetfulness is not good.

Nyanda   Please tell me who was the woman with the sharpest memory in the whole of Mokoba in our youthful days? In fact, in the whole of Ngawo chiefdom?

Jimui   It was Nyanda Jimui, my own Nyanda.

Nyanda   But now look at what age is doing to me, making me forget such a strange dream for

Fragile Rights/Frederick Bobor James

the whole day.

Jimui The night has not gone too far yet. Please tell me the dream before it is too late.

Nyanda Last night, you went with me to the farm to harvest my crops. Strangely, all the okra plants had borne eggplant fruits. They were shining on the trees like gold.

Jimui Did you touch them?

Nyanda I wanted to be sure they were eggplants. So I plucked one and tasted it. Even as I speak now, the taste has come fresh into my mouth.

Jimui Hey, eggplant fruits bearing on okra plants. That is an abomination!

Nyanda A tilapia cannot give birth to a catfish, that is what our people say.

Jimui We have to wait and see. It could be a good omen or a bad one. However, we don't have to discuss it with anyone. Lest the gossips pass it round the town. Some mouths are cursed and lack the blessings of God.

Fragile Rights/Frederick Bobor James

Nyanda   (*Njabu walks in and embraces Nyanda.*) Ah Njabu, what crime have we committed?

Njabu   Please, Mama, if anyone has committed a crime, it is me. (*Now shakes the hand of Jimui warmly.*)

Jimui   Please take a seat, my lovely daughter. I hope it is not bad news that has brought you here.

Njabu   (*Puts her hands on her chest.*) Oh my God, I do not know what to say. (*Both Nyanda and Jimui become agitated.*) I need help, though I am not in any trouble.

Jimui   Thank God. We are your parents, no matter what your book education tells you. Your father and I were not only born and brought up in the same village, but we joined the *Poro* society together. *Togbehs* are brothers of a special kind. Do not, therefore, hide your problem from us.

Njabu   My husband and I have become too busy now to do our housework before and after work. We need somebody to help us. We are prepared to pay that person well.

Nyanda   (*Laughs.*) If your "father" will allow me, I will help the whole day and come back

Fragile Rights/Frederick Bobor James

Jimui	home in the evening. What do you do in this house other than sitting here the whole day, narrating folk-tales?
Njabu	I was thinking of your youngest daughter. It would not feel right if my "mother' were to do this for me. Besides, I would want the person to live in with us.
Jimui	My daughter, it is you offering to help us, not the other way round. However, I want you to think again about your choice of helper.
Njabu	My husband and I are settled on the choice.
Jimui	My young daughter, I don't want pepper to bear on the okra plant that we are going to plant.
Njabu	I do not understand those wise words.
Jimui	I mean children of these days do not behave like their parents.
Nyanda	Their ideas are strange, and we do not want to be shamed.
Njabu	She is my sister; I will go the extra mile to put up with her. She will come to see you

Fragile Rights/Frederick Bobor James

Jimui	now and again. *(Calls their daughter.)* Gbessay? *(A young girl of about 19 years appears.)*
Gbessay	*(Kneels.)* Yes, Papa.
Jimui	You have been idling here, having dropped out of lower secondary school. Nothing much for you to do. You are going with your sister to help her with her house work. You hear me?
Gbessay	Papa, right now?
Jimui	Of course, right now. Now, now!
Nyanda	My dear husband, Gbessay needs to prepare herself. I am sure Njabu can give her two days to get ready.
Gbessay	Yes, Papa. I need to wash and iron my clothes and have my hair braided. My cousins would like to see a decent looking person join them.
Njabu	Two days will be fine with us. I will be right back to take her with me. *(Njabu leaves.)*
Jimui	Gbessay, please excuse us for a while. We have something private to discuss.

Fragile Rights/Frederick Bobor James

Nyanda (*As Gbessay leaves.*) Why did you talk about pepper bearing on okra plant?

Jimui As we spoke, your dream kept on coming to my mind.

Nyanda Men are known to keep tight lips on matters, but not you.

Jimui What are you afraid of here?

Nyanda You men are weak. Gbessay is young and attractive; anything can happen while she lives with those people.

Jimui Let us hope for the better. Please call Gbessay to join us.

Njabu Gbessay?

Gbessay Yes, Mama!

Nyanda Please join us for a moment.

Gbessay (*Appears and kneels as she talks.*) Papa, I am here, Mama I am here.

Jimui She is your daughter. Please warn her to behave herself while she lives with those people. Njabu's father and I are great friends. I would not want anything to spoil that relationship.

Nyanda Self-respect and a content mind should be your watchwords while you stay with the Kortumas. We are poor, but we hold our heads high up as we walk anywhere in Ngawo chiefdom. Your grandparents and parents have always protected the image of their family. That is what your father and I expect from you. Go and join your cousins the day after tomorrow. We expect the best behaviour from you.

Gbessay (*Kneels.*) I will do my best.

Light Goes Out.

Fragile Rights/Frederick Bobor James

ACT THREE, Scene Nine.

Tom *(Alone in the parlour.)* What is happiness? Money, children, kindred, power, good health, love or a happy marriage? *(Rises and walks towards the cupboard.)* Happiness is like the story of the six blind men who went to see the elephant. Great story! If you touch the tail, you feel a snake is in your hand. If you touch the ear, your happiness is a fan. You touch the leg and your happiness is a big mortar. *(Pours the wine and sipping.)* We are all blind men and women as far as happiness is concerned, especially in the marital home. No one can understand it all. Some men are poor, but they have beautiful children - boys and girls, and they have a happy marriage. They consider themselves happy. Others have all the money in the world, but can't buy cures for their diseases. Their happiness is gone with the wind. *(Takes a gulp.)* I have good education, money, two beautiful daughters, and married to one of the most beautiful women, with a good education. But am I happy? Is Thomas Joe Kortuma (TJK) happy? Before now, when my wife and I used to look at things in the same way, I was happy. But now, no. happiness, no more! *(Njabu walks in.)*

Fragile Rights/Frederick Bobor James

Njabu Tom, you are all alone in the parlour. Where is everyone?

Tom Hey, children, come and rejoice with me. Mummy is home early today. Come and tell me whether I should sacrifice a sheep, goat, or cow to mark the occasion. Please come. (*Embraces Njabu, but she struggles free.*)

Njabu Tom, you must stop embarrassing me in front of the children. This should not become a habit. (*The children run on stage and hug their mother.*)

Baindu Dad, let us sacrifice an elephant, one of the largest, if not the largest animal.

Fengeh No, a goat. You know the goat can eat an elephant, according to the last story Daddy told us. Mummy deserves a goat, not an elephant.

Njabu You see how stupid my children have become as a result of the lies you tell them in the name of stories?

Tom But their results do not portray them as stupid. They are on top of their class.

Njabu Baindu and Fengeh, you should be reading your books and not listening to stories told

Fragile Rights/Frederick Bobor James

          by your Dad.

Baindu   But Mummy, some of the books we read in school are full of stories. Stories that no one can believe. For example, stories like "Rabbit went to the market to buy Christmas gifts for her children and friends."

Tom   Njabu, you were going to bring a house maid after work today, where is she?

Njabu   The contact has been made, the young woman will be here the day after tomorrow.

Fengeh   (*Full of curiosity.*) Is she beautiful, Mummy? And friendly?

Baindu   Does she know how to cook well, Mummy?

Njabu   Let us wait and see. This is not the time to answer questions. I must rush and cook something for the family to eat (*Disappears into the bedroom.*)

Light Goes Out.

Fragile Rights/Frederick Bobor James

ACT THREE, Scene Ten.

Abie's Residence.

Fasia (*At table with Abie at 7:00pm.*) I have made up my mind, darling.

Abie: About what?

Fasia Our relationship.

Abie Yes?

Fasia I have no reliable partner to live with now, except you. Only you.

Abie Oh no, you cannot be serious.

Fasia I will come over as soon as you give me the green light. After that, I will ask for a divorce from my wife and you and I will marry.

Abie (*Puts down the spoon and fork and begins to look at the ceiling.*) It is not as easy as that, Fasia. I have no reason to live with you. We cannot go beyond our present relationship.

Fasia When I made the first offer you said it was too hot for your comfort, and now you are saying the second is too cold.

Abie (*Sobbing.*) My husband ran out on me five years ago. We had been married for only two years. We started like a couple that would last forever, but suddenly we began to misunderstand each other. Since he left, I have been empty and lonely in so many ways, in spite of you coming occasionally to chat and quarrel with me, and make me feel like a woman.

Fasia I am prepared to fill that gap for good.

Abie (*Screams.*) Oh, no! You cannot! Maybe you can, but you are another woman's husband. It will be wrong for me to snatch you from her.

Fasia Her attitude has pushed me out. I need refuge.

Abie Not here. Go back and be nice to her. Go and iron out your differences. You can both make it if you treat each other well. (*Yells.*) Please go! Go, go, and now!

Fasia (*Holds her in his arms.*) You need help, Abie. The state in which you are now, I cannot leave you alone and go.

Fragile Rights/Frederick Bobor James

Abie (*Leans on Fasia and begins to cry freely.*) Whatever you do now is not enough to clean up the image of men. Men drive many women crazy and put them on the warpath. You make them misfits, rejects. You make them unfulfilled.

Fasia I do not know what women want in this world. They own the men and their children. Maybe they want the whole world as well.

Abie We want less than that. We want our men to love, respect and hang heads with us. We want to be treated as equals, people that have rights and matter. We have brains just like them.

Fasia Equal with men?

Abie Of course!

Fasia We will try, in spite of the old cultural values.

Abie We will continue to fight for the rights of women. The day will come when you will all crumble under the pressure. (*Becoming hysterical.*) We will continue to fight, fight, and fight!
Light Goes Out.

Fragile Rights/Frederick Bobor James

ACT FOUR, Scene One.

Home of the Kortumas. A car pulls up and Njabu and Gbessay alight.

Njabu (*Njabu enters, hugs children and pats Tom lovingly on the back.*) Sorry, I am so late in coming home. I have someone with me. This is Gbessay, our maid. She will stay with us and go home now and again to see her parents. (*Tom eyes the girl closely.*)

Fengeh Mum, Gbessay is very pretty and young. We are going to like her. (*Leans on Gbessay.*)

Baindu (*Looking at Gbessay carefully.*) Mum, she will sleep in the same room with us?

Njabu (*Jokingly.*) From now on, she is going to be your second mother. We will sort out where she sleeps later. (*Children and Gbessay disappear into the children's room, carrying her bag with them. Njabu goes into their bedroom. Tom pours himself some whisky and is drinking it alone in the parlour.*)

Tom Njabu, will you join me in the parlour for a moment, please?

Njabu (*Joins Tom.*) Tom, I did not know you to

Fragile Rights/Frederick Bobor James

be an alcoholic.

Tom (*Walks to her and brings his head closer to hers.*) And I did not know you to be a bossy wife.

Njabu Bossy wife? Njabu, a bossy wife?

Tom Yes! Njabu, now dictating how this home should be run. Njabu, now separating herself from her children and husband, and handing their care over to a mere girl. (*Now walking away*). Njabu, gradually ceasing to be the loving woman I knew thirteen years ago. The innocent and quiet young woman who I promised on the altar to live with until death do us part (*Begins to shout.*) Why should I not drink for comfort? At night, our bedroom is invaded by a viper in your wild imagination. At night, Tom becomes a viper of whom Njabu is scared stiff.

Njabu (*Runs after him and puts her hand over his mouth.*) Tom, Tom, the children have just gone to bed. Also, I do not want this poor child who has just come, to know we have a problem between us. It will affect her.

Tom (*Gulps the rest of the drink and turns to look at Njabu squarely in the eye.*) How about my male child? The one who will take my family name into the third generation? When are we going to make him?

Njabu (*Angry.*) You are naïve and narrow-minded. If your two daughters become professional women before they marry, lawyers or medical doctors, they will retain their maiden names.

Tom How about the names of their children. I mean my grandchildren?

Njabu Something is wrong with some men, some African men. Why aren't you bothered about what happened to my own family name? I have lost it to you. Why should your children not lose theirs to other men? Besides, who determines the sex of the child, the mother or the father?

Tom I think I should have done better if I had married an illiterate woman, or one literate just enough to take care of my home. Now I understand why some men run away from highly educated women. See what Njabu is doing, giving me a lecture in biochemistry.

Njabu Coward, you want a woman who will say yes to everything you say, a woman without a brain.

Tom But what are married women for, if not to

Fragile Rights/Frederick Bobor James

| | obey their husbands? And Njabu, don't pretend you do not know what keeps the relationship between husband and wife alive. |

Njabu   Obedience in marriage should be a two-way street. The husband should obey the wife, just as the wife is expected to obey the husband. No one should be the boss, giving commands left and right.

Tom   (*He heads for more whisky.*) Now cast your mind back over the last thirteen years of our marriage, my dear Njabu. There was no distance between us, and there were no refusals. That way, peace and harmony were abundant. The idea of boss, no boss, never exsisted between us. Let us go back to where we started.(*As he takes the bottle, Njabu grabs his hand. Whilst they are struggling, the bottle falls off and breaks. Gbessay and the children run into the parlour.*) Please go back and sleep, nothing is wrong.

Gbessay   Please, let me sweep up the broken glass around the cupboard.

Njabu   The broom is in the kitchen.

As Gbessay goes for the broom, the light fades out.

Fragile Rights/Frederick Bobor James

ACT FOUR, Scene Two.

Two weeks later. At the home of the Kortumas; Gbessay brings the children home from school. Whilst they are busy eating snacks, Gbessay goes to the kitchen to cook.

Gbessay (*Singing "Love is the Answer" for a brief while.*) I hope *Misisi* and *Massah* are beginning to like my style of cooking. Today, I am preparing cassava leaves and broad beans, tomorrow potato leaves, and the day after okra sauce. This eating of plain soup or European food most of the time is not good enough. (*Continues to sing "Love is the Answer".*)

Tom (*Enters unnoticed, children rush to greet him.*) Good afternoon, my little darlings.

Chorus Good afternoon, Dad. We have come home early over the last two weeks, and cousin Gbessay is always very kind to us.

Tom Ah, that is good news. That is exactly why she is here. To make you people happy.

Baindu She must be making you and Mum happy too. She cooks very well. Real native food.

Fragile Rights/Frederick Bobor James

Gbessay (*As Tom moves towards his sleeping room, Gbessay walks in, kneels and greets him.*) Good evening, Massah.

Tom Good evening, my dear. What sauce are we having for dinner today?

Gbessay Cassava leaves.

Tom Ah, good to hear that. Did you add some broad beans to it?

Gbessay Enough of it, sir.

Tom Wonderful. (*As he disappears into the sleeping Room.*) I wonder if it was Gbessay I saw come and greet me just now. She is becoming refined very fast. Beautiful, cooks well, young, innocent and very dutiful. The children are beginning to accept and appreciate her. And above all, Njabu is becoming more and more distant. (*Tom enters the bedroom, leaves his computer bag there and joins the children in the parlour.*)

Baindu Dad, what is the new story today?

Tom Please bring the mat. This time it is about Spider and Monkey who were inseparable friends. These great friends fell out because

Fragile Rights/Frederick Bobor James

Fengeh	of food. (They spread the mat.) Only for food? Bananas?
Tom	No, it was rice, cooked rice.
Chorus	Do monkeys and spiders eat cooked rice like human beings?
Gbessay	(*Walks up to Tom and the children and kneels.*) Food is ready, *Massah*.
Tom	That is good news. Come on my queens, let us go and eat. If we have time after the meal, we will continue with the story. (*They go to the dining table, whilst Gbessay eats from the cooking pot in the kitchen.*)
Fengeh	Why does Gbessay always eat out of the pot? Why does she not join us at the table? After all, she does the cooking.
Tom	Custom does not allow Gbessay to sit with us at table.
Baindu	Is it that she does not know how to eat with fork and knife?
Tom	Even if she knows, she must not eat with us at table.
Baindu	What type of custom is this that discrimi-

Fragile Rights/Frederick Bobor James

Tom	nates against people? It is custom that treats people differently according to class. If you are a cook, you are a cook and should not eat with your bosses.
Baindu	Are Fengeh and I also her bosses?
Tom	By extension, yes.
Fengeh	Oh, wow! We did not know we were that important, did you, Baindu?
Baindu	You mean we belong to the class of important people? Stop dreaming.
Fengeh	But Gbessay can tell stories to us? Dad, she is a good storyteller. Her stories are not about spider but the cunning rabbit, women, children, etc.
Tom	Of course she may. You can go to your room now and listen to Gbessay tell stories until you sleep. (*As they rise to leave.*) Gbessay, please do not tell them any horror stories. Good night. (*The children kiss their Dad goodnight.*) This time I will drink beer. I have been having too much spirit lately. (*He walks to the freezer and takes out a pint of beer, pours it into a glass and sips.*) Ice cold, ah! This will calm me down. (*As he walks away from*

Fragile Rights/Frederick Bobor James

	the freezer, the door creaks and Njabu enters.)
Njabu	Good evening, Tom.
Tom	(Sarcastically.) Good evening, my boss.
Njabu	Please Tom, what is the reason for such sarcasm?
Tom	Just look at the time, my superior. It's past 10:00 pm. A married woman with young children, is this the time to come home from work?
Njabu	You know we are flying out tomorrow. We had to finish up all the arrangements for the trip today, and do an orientation.
Tom	Njabu, what time do you have left for your family? Tell me, what time do you have? Now, it is I who have to wait for you to come home before we close the doors. Is that right, Mr. Njabu? Tell me! *(Grabs her by the shoulders and shakes her vigorously.)*
Njabu	Oh my God! I am going to this Gender Conference with pains from my husband's violence all over my body. What progress are we making in our relationship with these ruffians?
Tom	Ruffians, let me show you who a ruffian is!

Fragile Rights/Frederick Bobor James

Njabu	*(Grabs her two hands, and she yells.)* Kill me, Tom, kill me! *(Gbessay rushes out from the children's room with a wrapper tied at her waist, her breasts exposed.)*
Gbessay	Please *Massah*, leave *Misisi*. I beg *Massah*, leave her.
Tom	*(Tom suddenly becomes aware of Gbessay's naked breasts, and relaxes his hold on Njabu.)* Gbessay, your business is to look after the children and not us.
Njabu	Next time make sure you are properly dressed before you come out of that room. *(She cups her breasts in both hands and goes into their room.)*

Light fades.

Fragile Rights/Frederick Bobor James

ACT FOUR, Scene Three.

At Abie's residence. The night before the trip to the Regional Conference.

Abie (*Fills a glass with wine, drinking and pacing.*) I think we are doing the right thing. And making the right impact. In spite of the conflicting ideas that few members bring to the meetings occasionally, and the gossip that we are paid good money for what we are doing, we are going to stand firm. I have just got the right person, Njabu. She is ready to give me all the support. And I can rely on her. (*Doorbell rings, she peeps, sees Fasia and opens.*) Why are you here? You should be home with your family.

Fasia Because you are flying out tomorrow.

Abie: Therefore?

Fasia I have come to say goodbye, though you did not invite me.

Abie The reason is that things always end on a sour note each time you come, and I want to leave here in a good frame of mind.

Fasia May I go to the kitchen and fix something

Fragile Rights/Frederick Bobor James

	for the two of us?
Abie	(*Laughs.*) Please don't be funny. You have never gone to the kitchen, why do you want to do it now?
Fasia	Open your doors to me and see how much I have changed.
Abie	I will bring a beer for you. You want to eat something first?
Fasia	Please, I'll start with the beer.

Light Goes Out.

Fragile Rights/Frederick Bobor James

ACT FOUR, Scene Four.

The Home of the Kortumas.

Gbessay (*Enters with the children from school in a very happy and relaxed mood.*) Go and leave your bags in the room, change into something casual, and then come and help me in the kitchen.

Baindu I will cook the sauce.

Fengeh I will cook the rice. (*The children go in to change.*)

Gbessay (*Talking to herself.*) They are girls, now is the time for them to start learning how to cook, if they are to make good housewives in the future. Some of us got our education from school, home; and the *Sande* society. I can see that these girls have only school, television, radio, and social media for their education. If I do not play my role very well, my cousins are going to miss out on their culture. Beautiful little things. It would be an historic day when they graduate from the *Sande* society. That day would be the tip of my service in the home of the Kortumas. Everyone would come and watch me dance my favourite *Sande* dance.

Fragile Rights/Frederick Bobor James

(Dances like a Sampa. The children come in and stand giggling at her. She suddenly sees them, stops dancing and begins to laugh.)

Baindu   Gbessay, you mean we have a celebration today and you did not tell us?

Gbessay   No celebration. I was just trying out the way I would dance on the day you angels graduate from the *Sande* society.

Fengeh   What is *Sande*?

Gbessay   *Sande*? It is the traditional school that our girls must attend before they grow up.

Baindu   What do they teach in that school?

Gbessay   In *Sande*, you learn what the home and your school cannot teach you.

Fengeh   Such as?

Gbessay   How to dance traditional dances, how to weave, how to look after your husband and children. Many other things!

Baindu   But today we do not have to attend *Sande* School to learn all that you have mentioned.

Gbessay   It is a crime to spy on the *Sande* Society.

Fragile Rights/Frederick Bobor James

Baindu But everything about *Sande* and what it teaches is in books and on the internet. In fact, there are strong international and national movements against *Sande*. They see it as the school for FGM.

Gbessay (*Shouts and puts her hands on her head.*) Kwo-o-o! Who taught this little girl about *Sande*? What has *Sande* done that it is being exposed left and right, and given all kinds of names?

Baindu In school they refer to FGM as a violation of the right of girls and women who are subjected to it.

Gbessay I cannot understand how a right issue comes into this.

Fengeh If you want to know more about the new English names for *Sande*, and how it violates the human right of women, you can discuss it with Mummy.

Gbessay Sorry. You people must be hungry now. What do you want to eat before we start cooking?

Baindu Fengeh, what would you like?

Fengeh Cornflakes, of course. It will give me a big

Fragile Rights/Frederick Bobor James

	appetite. I love to eat meals prepared by Gbessay.
Baindu	We will both have cornflakes. (*Whilst they are eating in the dining room, Gbessay is cooking in the kitchen.*)
Fengeh	Baindu, how do you like the *Sande* dance Gbessay was dancing just now?
Baindu	Fascinating, but very tough. If I dance like that for five minutes, I will faint.
Fengeh	I love the dance so much. The way she stretched and swayed both hands. As if swimming. She moved both legs in rhythm with the hands, and the head was slowly turning from left to right. With a perfect smile on her face.
Baindu	Will this dancing get you to join *Sande*?
Fengeh	Maybe there are other things one can learn in the *Sande*, but only in the secret society bush. Who knows?
Baindu	Do you think any of our parents would want us to join the *Sande*?
Fengeh	I don't know.

Fragile Rights/Frederick Bobor James

Baindu From their arguments, Mum will never think of sending us to *Sande* School. But Dad will. He will do it not because he is traditional, but to hurt and embarrass Mum.

Fengeh You are being too hard on Dad. You think he is the problem in this house?

Baindu They have both become problems of late. And there is no longer peace in this house. Do you know that?

Fengeh You think I am too young to know what is going on between them? They keep on blaming each other. But I think Mum should slow down on that organisation a little. The organisation, Dad and us, who must she put first?

Baindu Her children should be first, then Dad, and the organization last.

Febgeh Shall we tell Mum this, and try to bring peace to this house once and for all?

Baindu It will not be that simple. Mum will think Dad is brain washing us. She is too into her organisation right now.

Fengeh But don't you think we should try?

Fragile Rights/Frederick Bobor James

Baindu We have to. If we win, we win. If we fail, we fail. (*Gbessay calls them to join her in the kitchen.*)

Gbessay You have taken too long to join me in the kitchen. I have been waiting all along.

Fengeh (*As they join Gbessay in the kitchen.*) What sauce are we cooking this afternoon, Gbessay?

Gbessay All broad beans.

Fengeh (*Confused.*) What, all broad beans?

Gbessay Yes, all broad beans.

Baindu Gbessay, no! The last time Mum cooked that stuff, we could not eat it. It was very bitter.

Gbessay *Misisi* did not have sufficient time to prepare the beans well enough, perhaps. Wait and see, you will enjoy the sauce today.

Fengeh But Baindu and I are supposed to do the cooking toady?

Gbessay You need some time to learn from me. That is why I had to wait for you this long.

Fragile Rights/Frederick Bobor James

Baindu If you are not going to allow us to cook, we can as well go to the parlour and study.

Gbessay It is important for you to be around and watch. That way you will learn how to cook better than when you will learn it form cookery books.

Fengeh Gbessay, do you know how to prepare European dishes?

Gbessay European dishes? What are they?

Baindu Salad, macaroni, finger foods, that sort of thing.

Gbessay You eat them here?

Fengeh You started cooking African dishes on daily basis in this house.

Gbessay How can I prepare them when I don't even know what they are?

Baindu Do not worry, Mum will someday teach you how to prepare them. (*Tom presses the door bell and the children meet him at the door.*)

Tom How are my little queens doing today?

Chorus Oh, very well, Dad.

Fragile Rights/Frederick Bobor James

Tom How about Gbessay?

Baindu She has been teaching us how to cook, but she does not know how to prepare European dishes.

Gbessay (*Kneels to greet Tom.*) Good afternoon, *Massah*.

Tom The afternoon is not a good one.

Baindu Are you missing Mum, Dad?

Tom (*Smiles derisively.*) Your Mum, of course, I miss her a lot these days. But that is not the issue. I am a little unwell.

Baindu Have you seen a doctor?

Tom Come on, it is not that serious.

Gbessay *Massah*, hope you will get well soon. *Misis* should meet you as well as she left you.

Tom Of course she will meet me in good shape. (*Goes into their bedroom to change his dress.*)

Gbessay (*Gossiping.*) *Massah* is not well. Hope his condition will not get serious. His wife is not here to take him to hospital and to look after him. Could it be her absence that is making him sick? These black-white people, they love their partners as fish loves water. *Misisi,* you must come back soon before *Massah* gets very sick. (*Tom appears from the bedroom.*)

Tom My sweet darlings, let us go and see the wonders Gbessay has done with the food today. (*Now at the dining table eating and talking across to Gbessay who is in the kitchen.*) Gbessay, since you joined this house I have become overweight.. What magic are you playing with the food?

Gbessay (*Answers from the kitchen.*) No magic, *Massah*. As you are aware, African foods are heavy.

Tom That is true, we should start alternating them with some European foods.

Fengeh Gbessay cannot prepare European foods. She does not even know them.

Baindu Mummy will teach her.

Tom If your Mummy has the time. She will take some lessons at the Home Economics Centre nearest to us. (*They move from the dining room to the sitting room.*)

Fragile Rights/Frederick Bobor James

Fengeh Dad, today no storytelling. I have a test tomorrow.

Baindu So do I. (*They both go to their room to collect their books. Tom goes to the kitchen, casts a lustful glance at Gbessay as he passes by and takes a pint of beer from the freezer.*)

Tom (*On his way to the sitting room.*) Gbessay, do you feel happy being with us?

Gbessay Yes, *Massah*.

Tom: Good, we have to keep each other happy. You, us, and us, you.

Gbessay Yes, *Massah*. (*The children come back to the parlour with their books. Whilst they are studying, Tom goes into his room, but Gbessay joins them in the parlour.*) What are you having tests on tomorrow?

Fengeh Mathematics. But maths is my favourite subject. No worries, Gbessay.

Baindu Social Studies. I have been reading my notes over and over again.

Gbessay Very good. I will see who scores higher than the other.

Fragile Rights/Frederick Bobor James

Fengeh Me, of course. Mark my words, I always get hundred percent in all my mathematics tests and examinations.

Baindu If I get below hundred percent it will be for spelling mistakes. Even at that, I will not get below ninety percent.

Tom *(Comes back to the parlour. As soon as the children see him they start yawning.)* What, you have started yawning already? Gbessay, please help them to bed. After that, do come and massage me. *(Drinking and pacing.)* When a water beetle stops spinning, it ceases to be a water beetle. But is it not better for me to become a non-spinning water beetle than to spin in the wrong water? Being a non-spinning water beetle will not put me and my family to shame. My integrity will remain intact though not so much to the one who has set this trap for me. *(Sits on a chair and holds his head in both hands.)* What makes me a water beetle, if not spinning? But should I spin in every water? I hope the world can see the dilemma my wife has put me in. *(Gbessay comes back to the sitting room to join Tom, looking shy and hesitant.)* Take the mat and spread it in the corner over there. *(Tom lies on the mat.)* Come on, please come and massage me.

Fragile Rights/Frederick Bobor James

Gbessay (*Politely reluctantly.*) *Massah*, please let me call the children to come and…

Tom Sssh! (*Gbessay moves close.*) Sit down and feel relaxed.

Gbessay *Massah*, I don't know how to….

Tom Just press my legs, my back, and my waist – gently. (*Gbessay now massaging.*) Your touch relaxes my muscles and makes my blood flow freely.

Gbessay (*Scared.*) *Massah*, please.

Tom I mean my muscles are all cramped, and my knees ache when I walk. The pain comes right up to my waist and to my neck. (*Holds Gbessay by the hand and moves it towards his waist.*) Press my waist. Use both hands, and do it gently. That is where my illness lies. (*As Gbessay presses.*) Gently, please.

Gbessay *Massa*h, it is enough. I should join the children now. They must wake up and see me with them in the room. (*About to move away.*)

Tom (*Seizes Gbessay by the hand.*) I have something to tell you which I do not want the children

	to hear. Please follow me. *(Leading Gbessay towards his bedroom.)*
Gbessay	Please *Massah*, here too can be a suitable place to tell me this secret. The children are already sleeping.
Tom	Come on, be a pleasant little friend to me. I have been miserable since…
Gbessay	*(Surprised.)* How can you be miserable with all these riches? Two beautiful daughters, a loving wife, and a good job.
Tom	Let us go, not all that glitters is gold. Our people say that even the goat sweats, but it is the fur that hides the sweat. *(The front door bell rings as Tom and Gbessay approach the bedroom door).* Please go to your room. I will go and see who is at the door. *(Opens the door).* Come on, you cannot say you have been in this city and our paths do not cross.
Fasia	My brother, problems. Economic and social problems, made worse by the new problem of gender equality.
Tom	What do you drink?
Fasia	I don't mind a cold beer.

Fragile Rights/Frederick Bobor James

Tom (*Going for the beer.*) Ma-a-an! The problems with gender equality are not unique to one home nowadays. Our modern women are on the warpath. They are fighting a gender war.

Fasia They pursue the rights of women at the expense of all other rights: the rights of the men, and the children, for example. That is the problem with them.

Tom (*Offers Fasia the drink.*) To me it is superiority they want, not equality.

Fasia This war has ruined my marriage. My wife insists on us sharing the chores. If she cooks the sauce, I should cook the rice. She wants us to share the housework on a 50/50 basis.

Tom Your wife is not alone in this. There is a new school which teaches them this confusion! My family is in ruins at the moment. It is a disaster.

Fasia I thought I was suffering this new husband-wife relationship alone.

Tom As you can see, my wife is not even in the country. When she is in the country, she

Fragile Rights/Frederick Bobor James

comes home very late in the evening.

Fasia My brother, if I find a suitable place to run to, I will desert my home. My wife will then look for another man to control.

Tom: (*Laughs.*) Don't run away. That will be unmanly. You should not run away from the dance because you find the style of dancing unbearable. That is what our people say.

Fasia But tell me, apart from this gender equality stuff, what else is responsible for the crisis in modern homes today? As you are aware, there are far too many broken homes.

Tom Socio-economic freedom. If they were illiterate, not earning wages, just staying at home and looking after the children together with their cowives, there will be fewer problems.

Fasia (*Laughs.*) The scenario you have painted is no longer tenable in our own generation. You know that. You will be branded as an enemy of development.

Tom What is the best solution to this ugly situation?

Fragile Rights/Frederick Bobor James

Fasia I think the time has come for us to start accepting some of the conditions put forward by our wives. We need peace, we cannot be at loggerheads with them all the time.

Tom The solution is, the gender movement groups need to know that change is a gradual process.

Fasia You are right. There is bound to be tension in any home where the wife forces this change down the husband's throat.

Tom My wife has been forcing the change down my throat in large morsels. Swallowing it has been unbearable for me.

Fasia We will get there with time. It is a long and rugged road.

Tom Sometimes I feel like going to the kitchen to cook, clean the house, and wash all our dirty linens in the name of peace and unity in this house.

Fasia But what is stopping you, Tom? You will be the best modern husband, a role model, and the darling of your wife.

Tom But Fasia, imagine that my children wake

Fragile Rights/Frederick Bobor James

	up one morning and find Daddy sweeping the compound, or my father comes for a visit and meets his Thomas in the kitchen cooking for the family.
Fasia	You and I may decide to brave these cultural absurdities, but our people say that it is gradual steps that take the sparrow to the dust bin.
Tom	Small steps my brother, not a push-pull.
Fasia	(*Rises to go.*) I was passing by and decided to drop in for a chat.
Tom	This has been a very useful discussion, my brother. You have lifted some load from my mind.

Light Goes Out.

Fragile Rights/Frederick Bobor James

The Next Day.

Gbessay returns home with the children from school.

Gbessay (*While the children are walking across the parlour.*) Please come and eat after you have changed.

Fengeh You did not wait for us to help you cook today?

Gbessay There is much time for that. We have to eat early because *Massah* is taking us to the beach shortly after he comes home.

Baindu Ah yes, now I remember. We are going to the beach!

Fengeh (*Raises a fist.*) Ah yes! To the beach! (*Tom enters.*)

Chorus Dad, we are eating and going to the beach?

Tom Yes, and we are going with Gbessay, all right?

Chorus Yes, Dad, we will love to have Gbessay around. (*Tom joins the children at the dining table.*)

Fragile Rights/Frederick Bobor James

Baindu What does the sea look like, Dad?

Tom Ah, the sea. It is very big and rough.

Fengeh You make me fear the sea already, Dad. Big and very rough?

Tom That is right. The sea is rough. But not all the time. There are times when it is calm.

Baindu Will it be calm this evening, so that we can learn how to swim?

Tom We will know when we get there.

Fengeh Do you know how to swim, Dad? Someone has to teach us how to swim.

Tom In fresh water, yes. But I have not tried the sea.

Fengeh You are a coward, Dad. Once you can swim in fresh water, you can swim in the sea, too.

Tom That is what you think. I think differently.

Baindu Who normally goes to the beach, and why?

Tom The beach is for everyone. Different people go there for different reasons. The fish mongers go to the beach to buy fish from the fishermen. The rich go there to enjoy their money.

Fengeh What group do we belong to, Dad?

Tom Today we belong to both groups. We will enjoy ourselves, and buy some fish for the house.

Baindu But Gbessay will buy the fish, not us.

Tom We are running late. Let us leave, now! *(The kids and Gbessay rush into their room and come back to the parlour with a bag and two mats. They giggle as they run to the vehicle outside.)*

Light Goes Out.

Fragile Rights/Frederick Bobor James

ACT FOUR, Scene Six.

Just after the trip to the beach.

Fengeh	Dad, I am so tired that I feel like going straight to bed.
Baindu	So am I.
Tom	Not before everyone has told me what was her most exciting experience at the beach.
Baindu	That is better than telling stories.
Tom	Now let us start. Mama Fengeh, tell us your most exciting experience at the beach this evening.
Fengeh	I was fascinated by that angry sea rushing onto the bank, but stopping almost at the same point each time it came. I think it was afraid of the huge crowd that was on the beach today.
Baindu	I have never heard a stupid talk such as this. The sea afraid of people? Go and stand in its way, then you will know if it is afraid of people or not.
Tom	Why are you interfering with her own experience? Now, you go ahead and tell us

Fragile Rights/Frederick Bobor James

	your own findings.
Baindu	I actually put some of the sea on my tongue to find out if it is true that it is salt water, as people say. I wonder who salted that massive water, and where he/she got all the salt from.
Tom	You are both very curious animals. Now go and bathe, come and eat something and then go to bed. (*As they disappear.*) Gbessay, what is there to eat? I mean something light.
Gbessay	I fried plantains and potatoes before we left for the beach.
Tom	Lovely. (*Whispers.*) What will you do for me after the kids have gone to bed?
Gbessay	*Massah*, please. This question makes me very nervous.
Tom	(*Smiles at her broadly.*) Massage? That soothing caress froom your fingers, they make me long for more.
Gbessay	You are dragging me too far into this massage game. It is bound to lead us into trouble.
Tom	It is the goat's favourite leaf that gives it a

Fragile Rights/Frederick Bobor James

running stomach. (*Rises from the seat and stretches.*) Maybe it will give me colic. Me, running stomach? No. (*Kids emerge from their room.*)

Tom You mean you have bathed already?

Baindu Call it dry cleaning. We only needed to shake the sand off our bodies.

Tom To the dining table everyone. We need to have a bite of something. I am sure my queens are hungry now.

Fengeh (*All at table, but Gbessay.*) Dad, you should take us to the beach every evening.

Tom Every evening? You know that is impossible.

Baindu How about Saturdays, Dad?

Tom That sounds okay, though I will make no promise.

Fengeh If you can't, Mummy will take us there.

Tom You think your Mum has time for family these days?

Baindu (*Raises her voice for Gbessay to hear from the*

Fragile Rights/Frederick Bobor James

	Kitchen.) If the two of you cannot, I am sure Gbessay will. Will you Gbessay, please?
Gbessay	(*Raises her voice from the kitchen.*) Yes, *Massah*?
Tom	Your cousins are asking that you take them to the beach every Saturday evening.
Gbessay	With your permission, *Massah*, it will be done.
Tom	We will know with time, if it can fit into our programme.
Baindu	I think going to the beach once a week will not be too much.
Fengeh	The next time we are there, I will swim.
Baindu	I prefer to fish. I will need a hook and line.
Tom	There is need for swimming and fishing lessons for the two of you.
Fengeh	I think you and Gbessay need swimming lessons, too. We should all dive into the sea and swim as a family. If one is being carried away by the sea, the others will help.
Tom	(*As the children rise to go to bed, Tom goes to the cupboard to pour himself some whisky.*) Good

Fragile Rights/Frederick Bobor James

night and sleep well, my queens.

Chorus Sleep well too, Dad. (*The track "Love is the Answer" plays as Gbessay packs the table. Tom now sits on the mat, drinking. Gbessay joins him after packing.*)

Tom I promised I would tell you the cause of my misery here in this house. But start massaging me first. This time begin with the back of my neck.

Gbessay (*Massaging freely.*) Each time you ask me to massage you, I think of my grandfather. He was fond of asking us, the grandchildren, to massage him.

Tom This time you should think of a young man who is lonely and miserable. And needs companionship.

Gbessay Don't be ungrateful to God. You have a young and loving wife, and two beautiful daughters. You also have money.

Tom I have a wife, yes. But she does not belong to me anymore. She has given her love and time to an organisation.

Gbessay An organisation? What kind of organisation?

Fragile Rights/Frederick Bobor James

Tom The one that has taken her away to another country for ten days. An organisation to give more power to women over men.

Gbessay How can women be more powerful than men? That is impossible.

Tom Now she has brought you here to take care of the children, and make me happy. (*He puts his hand on Gbessay's shoulder. She takes it off and puts it down gently.*) Let us go into the room over there, away from the hearing of the children, I will tell you the rest of the story. (*They rise, as they get to the door, the main doorbell rings. Tom goes there as Gbessay rushes to her own room. Njabu enters.*) Welcome. Why do you come surprising us like a thief?

Njabu The conference was cut short by one day, and you know the problem with flights in our subregion. (*She pulls the bag across the parlour.*) How is everybody?

Tom If you thought we would starve whilst you were away, you were wrong.

Njabu Tom, please don't make this place hell for me. I am just coming home after being away for nine days. (*As Njabu drags the bag into the room, Tom goes for whisky.*) All you do in this house now is create surprises,

	unpleasant surprises. By the way, what have you been doing in the parlour, when everybody is in bed?
Tom	Praying fervently for you to come back, and a changed woman.
Njabu	Praying or swimming in brandy?
Tom	Call it what you may. (*They both disappear into the bedroom, and the light goes off for a brief interval. When the light comes on again, Njabu runs back to the parlour. Tom follows her shortly after.*)
Njabu	What game is this again, Tom? Why do you prick me with a sharp object when I am about to sleep? Why Tom, why?
Tom	What, Njabu? Why do you run away from the bedroom shouting?
Njabu	You know why Tom, you know. You pricked me with a sharp object when I was just about to sleep. You know very well that I have just come back from a trip, extremely tired.
Tom	But why will I prick you, Njabu?
Njabu	(*Shouting.*) Come on Tom, don't be funny. Who else can do that to me when there are

Fragile Rights/Frederick Bobor James

	just the two of us in our bedroom?
Tom	(*Plaintively.*) You shout at me now, Njabu, don't you? You do not even know now that I am your husband?
Njabu	Because you do not respect my privacy. Your only concern is your right to your wife at night. Even when I am tired. From tomorrow we are going to live in separate rooms. We will meet when it is absolutely necessary.
Tom	Good! That will be suitable for our relationship. From that time on, you will go and come when you like. In fact, I will give you your own set of keys to the doors.
Njabu	(*Begins to pace the parlour, away from Tom.*) Yes, maybe that will lessen the tension between us.
Tom	(*Looking at the ceiling, and pacing in a different Direction.*) When faeces are found in a public place, no one takes responsibility for them. (*Begins to laugh derisively.*)
Njabu	(*Rushes at Tom, grabs his two hands and begins to shake him vigorously.*) Tom, Tom! I am sure you are not going mad. No, you are not! First, like a little boy, you pricked me just

Fragile Rights/Frederick Bobor James

now when we were in bed and denied knowledge of it, and now you are laughing deliriously.

Tom (*Turns suddenly, frees himself from Njabu's grip and he in turn grabs her two hands.*) If this place has suddenly become a hell, you are the cause. (*Shaking her.*) Before now, you loved me, and I loved you. Our children were our treasure. We observed each other's rights. That way our love for each other overflowed, and this place was bursting with happiness.

Njabu (*Struggling to break free from Tom.*) The fact is that, I have put you down from my back. I have told you, "You, my baby no more."

Tom (*Shaking her.*) Baby, eh? You will soon learn that you are dealing with a grown up, and the head of this family.

Njabu (*Frees herself from Tom's grip, runs for a knife and puts Tom in a helpless position.*) Tom, I cannot understand why, like most men, you won't change. Where has all your Western education gone?

Tom (*Shows Njabu his throat.*) My equal partner. No, my superior! Here, cut my throat and offer me as sacrifice for the prosperity of

Fragile Rights/Frederick Bobor James

	your movement. Go on, kill me. Go ahead, kill me.
Njabu	(*Knife falls off her hand, and she embraces Tom and weeps.*) Tom, my wedding vow was not to cut your throat. I vowed to be your better half.
Tom	(*Looking at the ceiling.*) You vowed to be my better half, but now you are my tormenting bigger half. (Tom begins to laugh, feverishly this time).
Njabu	(*Withdraws suddenly and begins to shout.*) Hell! We are never prepared to compromise our position. You have to respect my rights. We have made resolutions at the conference, and we are going to pursue them to the end. (*Runs to the right corner of the parlour, screaming.*)
Tom	(*Walks slowly to the opposite corner, shaking his head.*) I know none of us has gone mad. But if anyone of us has, it is you, Njabu. You are violating a lot of norms in pursuit of your so-called rights.
Njabu	(*Turns in the direction of Tom.*) Yes, rights that had been buried, and we are sacrificing everything to exhume. *Light Goes Out.*

Fragile Rights/Frederick Bobor James

ACT FOUR, Scene Seven.

Scene Changes to Abie's Residence.

Abie (*Comes dragging her luggage across the parlour from the Regional Gender Conference. Looks around the parlour slowly.*) Coming to a lonesome home is always a dreadful feeling. It sometimes makes me want to build a golden stool in my heart for Fasia. (*Shakes her head violently*). But no! Such a seat will make my heart give in to the gimmicks of the menfolk.
(*Disappears with the bag into her bedroom. She returns to the parlour shortly after and finds a letter on the floor. She opens it, pours herself a drink and begins to look at it dimly. The content is intoned by a male voice on a CD player.*)

Dear Abie,
I am writing to you on behalf of the Belia family to express our disappointment that while everyone says that salt is tasty, you spit it out and say it is bitter. We are gravely concerned that you have not only decided to live without a family, but that you have opened and led a school that teaches other woman how not to live in harmony with their husbands. I now understand why if some families have to choose between sending their boy or girl to school, they will choose to send the boy. (*As the voice fades*

away, she gets up and walks away slowly from the table, and begins to mimic the content of the letter.) 'While everyone says that salt is tasty, you spit it out and say it is bitter." But cannot they see the many bitter sides of the proverbial tasty salt? The repercussion it has had on the African woman and development in Africa? *(Screams.)* Oh no! We have had too much of the proverbial tasty salt. *(Almost shouting.)* Tell me, what is good about FGM, early marriage, teenage pregnancy, polygamy, unplanned families, violence against women, high illiteracy rate among women, high infant mortality and morbidity rates in most African countries? *(Weeping.)* What are my parents telling me in this stupid letter? Sit down Abie, and watch all of these ills against the women go on unchecked? *(Shouting the words.)* Oh no! Never! This battle will continue unabated! *(Fasia enters unexpectedly. In a harsh tone.)* What have you come to do here? *(Looking at Fasia angrily in the face, with Fasia looking back in surprise.)* Come on, tell me, or I show you the door.

Fasia Look, Abie, let me be brutally frank with you today. It is better to stay married and demonstrate how equality with men can be achieved. By living singly and fighting your cause, you are behaving like an estranged trade unionist. Are you an example for others to copy?

Abie (*Collapses into Fasia's arms.*) You are always here to make me feel helpless, Fas.

Fasia I simply want you to pursue your goal in the right way. That is, man and woman living amicably in partnership. Where is your example?

Abie If I have to be in matrimony to fight the cause of women, it does not have to be with you. You are a big stumbling block, by all indications.

Light Goes Out.

Fragile Rights/Frederick Bobor James

ACT FOUR, Scene Eight.

Home of the Kortumas.

Gbessay (*Talking in her sleep.*) Grandma, you died several years ago. What have you come to do here?

Ghost (*Nasalized voice.*) I have brought this child for you.

Gbessay Child? What will I do with a child at this time in my life? You know my position in this family, a mere servant.

Ghost Fear not, this is a male child. This family has been in need of one for a long time. You are going to be the hen that lays the golden egg.

Gbessay Golden egg? What right do I have to lay a golden egg in people's house? Who will own and care for the hen and the chicken when it is hatched?

Ghost Do not worry about that. The house is owned by someone. He will own and care for the chicken when it is hatched. Here I leave him with you, Gbessay. Take him, I say, take him.

Gbessay Did our people not say that one cannot

Fragile Rights/Frederick Bobor James

claim a scarecrow that he has erected on somebody's farm?

Ghost How can you become part of the farm without pitching something there?

Gbessay (*Half-awake now.*) Little boy, please follow the one who has brought you here. Grandma, Grandma! Please come and take him away; do not leave him behind to suffer. Please do not do that to him. He is a pleasant little thing.(*Shouting now.*) Come back Granny, please come and take him away. I say come back, I am not ready for any trouble.

Ghost Your people here live in a selfish world. What is wrong with you becoming *Tomosi's* second wife and officially warming his bed and increasing the number of his children?

Gbessay But Grandma, it has to do with rights.

Ghost Rights? How can you feed a child without licking your fingers? Selfishness! (*Ghost disappears.*)

Tom (*Comes running towards Gbessay's room and stops at the door.*) Come on Gbessay, what is the matter with you? With whom are you

	conversing? I could hear a very strange voice in conversation with you.
Gbessay	(*Emerges from the room trembling*) A dream, I was dreaming.
Tom	Are you alright?
Gbessay	(*Still trembling.*) Yes, I am.
Tom	This dream, can you tell me a bit of it?
Gbessay	(*Stammers.*) No, I, I will not. Please.
Tom	Well, go back in and sleep. Good night.
Gbessay	Good night, *Massah*. (*They both depart to their different rooms.*)

Light Goes Out.

Fragile Rights/Frederick Bobor James

ACT FOUR, Scene Nine.

Meeting of the WLM Inner Circle.

Abie (*An air of anxiety hangs in the meeting room.*)
This meeting is your brainchild, Daisy.
We have never had an inner circle meeting
before. Why have you called for one now?

Daisy (*Clears her throat.*) An agama lizard does not
rest on the the same stump all the time for
nothing. I have the feeling that the battle
we are fighting is taking a toll on some
front commanders. What we have
embarked on is about teaching old dogs
new tricks. And that is not going to happen
overnight. There is a need for us to re-
examine our strategy. The question we need
to ask ourselves is "Are we making impact,
or making our targets dig in more and
more?" We need to …

Abie From your outbursts at meetings, I have
always seen treachery in your eyes. Has
anyone of us complained to you? Are you
merely going around sniffing the air in
members' compounds, trying to find out if
there is trouble smelling there? Or you are
just a big gossip?

Fragile Rights/Frederick Bobor James

Daisy Abie, if the one who means well for this movement and her members is a gossip, I will be most happy to be referred to as one.

Mbetu Abie, there is no need for tempers here. Except if those who this cap fits are trying to wear it.

Njabu *(Weeping quietly.)* I think we should listen to Daisy patiently.

Mbetu If you are busy looking for a speck in other people's eyes, you will not even know when you have a log in your own eye. I am sure Daisy is asking for introspection.

Daisy *(Continues.)* For three nights now I have had the same dream. The woman in the dream faces a great challenge in her married home. Things fall apart for her, her husband, and children every single night the dream replays itself. I see it as a premonition for us all.

Abie *(A bit tense.)* Some of us, before we fall into the river, we take off our outer garments so that we can swim unhindered. What is this garbage about a dream? I say go back to the bank and take off your outer garments and then plunge into the river, fellow swimmers. We must not allow superstition to derail the gains we have made.

Mbetu I think our goal is not reckless, naked swimming that will lead us to headlong collision with the sharks in the deep. We want to swim across the sea of male chauvinism unhindered. We therefore need to apply maximum tact in doing so.

Njabu Should we not live by example? Practise what we preach? Should we be hypocrites? Tell our womenfolk what to do, and then we do the opposite? Someone, please tell me. What are the rules? Maybe some of us are going too fast. (*Breaks down.*) Yes, perhaps we are jumping without looking and asking how high.

Abie (*Puts her hands around Njabu and they begin to sob.*) I am sure you are ready to stand by me. If they all run away, you and I will stay and fight this fight together. We do not have to think too much about what it will cost us.

Njabu We have to be prepared for the cost, if we have to win this battle. True, only a foolish and reckless General goes to war without considering the cost of losing or winning.

Light Goes Out.

Fragile Rights/Frederick Bobor James

ACT FIVE, Scene One.

At the home of the Kortumas. Tom is sleep walking.

Tom *(Tom opens the bedroom door and walks into the sitting room, with Njabu following him quietly.)* When you and I were growing up, were there not clearly defined roles? Roles for males and for females? Were we not all taught our roles? On the farm, did the boys not help their male parents to brush the farm, fell the trees, burn the farm, clear and plough? Did our sisters not help their female parents to cook for the males while they worked on the farm? Did our sisters not go fishing to provide additional protein for the family meal? When we were going to school, did the pattern change? No! The boys continued to do male tasks and the girls female tasks in school, too. That continued in this home for a while and it continues in many peaceful modern homes even today. (*His voice trembles.*) For me, it wasn't until my wife joined that divisive female club; or shall I say that anti-male, goddamned club that is eating deep into my family. Eating away at the peace and happiness of my innocent daughters and keeping my wife aloof…

Fragile Rights/Frederick Bobor James

Njabu   Oh Tom, you have been so troubled by my so called commitment to WLM that you go to bed with it, sleepwalk with it, and wake up with it at dawn. You have to be careful that it does not knock you off one fine day.

Tom   (*Tom is startled and starts smacking his back without turning to look.*) Please get off my back and allow me to sleep. Witch, you harass me in the day and at night too. Allow peace to come into my life, for God's sake.

Njabu   You are walking and talking in your sleep. (*Shaking Tom now.*) Wake up and see where you are?

Tom   (*Tom turns around, sees Njabu and then begins to take in his surroundings.*) Is this what you do when you come back home tired and fall asleep? In your deep sleep you monitor me to know if I am breathing properly or not, if I am dreaming and walking in my sleep or not? If you pester me to death, I know you will follow me into the next world to make sure I do not have peace there, too.

Njabu   Who is nagging who in this house, Tom? Who is suppressing the rights of the other? Who is shouting and disrupting the peace of this family every day and night? Tell me, Tom, who is the nuisance of this house?

Fragile Rights/Frederick Bobor James

Tom Whether I am the rabble rouser or not; go back to sleep and leave me alone. Leave me alone to sleepwalk until I have cleared the venom from my chest. Until I have cleared the delirium from my head. (*Pushing her gently.*) Please go. Go and leave me alone.

Njabu (*Going to their bedroom.*) I am worried about you, Tom. This is simple madness. There are far better things to do than ruminating and yelling about one thing all the time.

Tom (*Raising his voice a little.*) If you worry about me, I will know. Without you broadcasting it on the national radio. O, so many things have gone wrong with me, eh? You, you mean so many things? (*Heads for the bedroom.*)

Light Goes Out.

ACT FIVE, Scene Two.

Nine months later. Tom and Gbessay at the Beach.

Tom (*Lying on his back on a mat, with Gbessay sitting close and massaging his legs.*) I always feel safe alone with you here on the beach. Oh, how I wish I could afford a beach house where we could hide from the bickering of Njabu. A beach house with a posh porch where we could sit and watch the sea roll and splash on the bank. Where we could sit close together and watch the pelicans fly back home from the day's search for food, watch the fishermen returning with boat loads of their catch, and the red setting sun gliding over the sea.

Gbessay Enough of fantasy, *Massah*. We should....

Tom I have told you time and again not to "*Massah*" me when we are alone together.

Gbessay Tom, we should be talking about the present state I am in, and not fantasies.

Tom I am still the master of my house, in spite of the challenges posed to my authority by my wife. Your child will be called Kortuma and it will have equal rights as its sisters. In fact,

Fragile Rights/Frederick Bobor James

	more rights if it turns out to be a male.
Gbessay	How about me? Will I have a place in your home after that, even as a maid?
Tom	You will be elevated. You will be my paramour, and will enjoy more privileges than my conceited wife whose head has of late been full of power. Women's power.
Gbessay	*(Sobbing.)* Tom, we are talking about rights here. What right have I to have a child by you? What rights will an illegitimate child have among legitimate children? How can you make me a second wife? *(Pause.)* Paramour, you said. How can the rights of a paramour compare with those of a wife? *(Rises from the mat and begins to walk away.)* In the traditional setting, it will pose no problem for me. But in this modern setting where rights are magnified, I wonder what my fate is going to be. I wonder, I wonder. *(Tom, who has been following Gbessay quietly, puts his hands around her.)*
Tom	We all have rights. No matter where we are, and what we are. But rights are so fragile that we have to be careful when it comes to exercising them. No one has the right to use his or her rights like a blade, to cut through the rights of others.

Fragile Rights/Frederick Bobor James

Gbessay Can my rights be matched against those of my *Misisi*? I am a woman quite all right, but of inferior breed and with subservient rights. They cannot stand the test of modernization. How can you use sword rights against machine-gun-rights?

Tom Rights are equal; we talk about equal rights these days. That is what Njabu and others preach every day, though theirs are skewed in favour of the elites.

Gbessay But how can the rights of a maid and those of her mistress compare? Tell me, Tom. (*She begins to weep.*)

Light Goes Out.

Fragile Rights/Frederick Bobor James

ACT FIVE, Scene Three.

Home of the Kortumas. Gbessay returns from the market and is cooking.

Gbessay (*In the kitchen cooking, and singing. After a while she feels a sharp pain, sits down and rests her head on her right palm.*) O God, things have moved so fast with me in this house. What a sharp pain in my tummy! And at once I feel so sick, weak and full of nausea. If I am dying God, wait until I deliver my baby. Please God, please. (*She collapses on the floor, and Njabu arrives on the scene one minute or so after.*)

Njabu (*Rushes to Gbessay as soon as she sees her on the Floor.*) Gbessay, Gbessay! (*Feeling her pulse and the children join her from their room*). What? She needs medical attention right now. My God, what can I do? (*Calls the hospital.*)

Light goes out.

Fragile Rights/Frederick Bobor James

ACT FIVE, Scene Four.

At the Hospital.

Doctor (*After removing the corset Gbessay is wearing, and examining her.*) This young lady is pregnant and can deliver at any time now.

Njabu What did you say, doctor?

Doctor This young woman is expecting a baby.

Njabu (*Furious and confused.*) No, doctor! You cannot tell me that. How can she be pregnant all this time, and I do not know?

Doctor (*Shows Njabu the corset Gbessay has been Wearing.*) You can see that she has been using a corset. That way she has been able to conceal the pregnancy from people.

Njabu (*Puts her hand on her chest.*) My God, this is devious! How did it happen? And who is behind this? Gbessay, who is the father of that child you have been compressing in that womb?

Gbessay (*Weakly.*) I don't know.

Njabu You mean you have been going out with

	several men? Even that, you should be able to know who the father of your child is.
Gbessay	(*Shouts and closes her eyes.*) O-o my mother, I am dying in your absence. My dear mother, please come and be present while I die.
Doctor	Madam, please excuse us, this woman is in labour. Subjecting her to this kind of questioning will not help her. (*Njabu leaves reluctantly, whilst Gbessay is carried to the labour room.*)

*Light goes out, when it comes on, Njabu is standing restlessly in the corridor of the Maternity war*d.

Njabu (*Calls Tom at his office.*) Hello, Tom, yes. Njabu here. Tom, I am at the hospital, Cottage! Gbessay is in labour. It is true, okay, quickly, please. (*Talking to herself now.*) This is beyond my imagination. How did it happen? Our people say that a female sheep can get pregnant without contact with a male sheep. Once it is exposed to the dew. Certainly, there is a mysterious dew behind this pregnancy. Njabu is going to go all out to unearth this mystery. Njabu will know when the dew fell on Gbessay, and where? (*Tom arrives from a different direction unnoticed.*)

Fragile Rights/Frederick Bobor James

Tom Njabu, is it true?

Njabu Today is not April 1, Tom. It is real.

Tom Oh, God! What is all this?

Njabu Don't worry, Tom. We will go all out to know who the culprit is. These are the kinds of issues WLM is good at handling?

Tom What are you driving at now?

Njabu WLM will get the father of the child and force him to take responsibility for both mother and child.

Tom We will pay Gbessay off and send her back home, period.

Njabu Then she will add to the number of misplaced women we have in our country, and her child will swell the number of unwanted children out there on the street.

Tom This is no place for a lecture on gender, and the plights of women. (*A nurse opens the door to the labour room and the voice of a baby is heard crying.*) What did she bring?

Nurse A baby boy and he is as handsome as his uncle here. (*Closes the Labour Room.*)

Fragile Rights/Frederick Bobor James

Tom (*Jumps inadvertently.*) Good Jesus, a baby boy! (*Suddenly realizes his mistake.*) Don't you think we should allow that boy to grow with our children?

Njabu Not until we know who his father is. Until such a time, Gbessay is going back to her parents.

Tom You must not take a decision on the fate of this child alone. (*Njabu is too confused to digest the reactions of Tom.*)

Light fades.

Fragile Rights/Frederick Bobor James

ACT FIVE, Scene Five.

At Abie's Residence.

Abie (*Watching TV. Suddenly, Fasia appears dragging his luggage into the parlour.*) What is this? Why are you coming here with all your belongings?

Fasia I cannot live with my wife any longer. If you cannot have me here, tell me. I will look for a cheap guesthouse where I can stay until I sort myself out.

Abie Fas, you have to move into a guesthouse. I cannot afford to accommodate you in here.

Fasia How about tonight?

Abie You should go and leave your things somewhere, and then come back.

Light Goes Out.

Fragile Rights/Frederick Bobor James

ACT FIVE, Scene Six.

At the home of the Jimuis. Gbessay is being interviewed by Njabu.

Njabu Gbessay, if you have to come back and work for us after your child has become strong enough, we have to know who his father is.

Gbessay Your husband will be in a better position to tell you who the father of my child is. (*Njabu stands over the child and looks at him thoroughly.*)

Njabu (*Rushing out.*) What an ugly situation is this?

Jimui (*Confused.*) If only she had listened to us.

Nyanda How could she, we are illiterate and backward.

Jimui We are illiterate, but we have each seen the sun rise and fall more times than the two of them put together.

Gbessay You are right, but you have not seen the sun rise and fall in Europe or America, and in winter.

Fragile Rights/Frederick Bobor James

Jimui If I were you, I would just shut up. Shameless fool!

Gbessay With the pressure I was under, no woman could have done better.

Light Goes Out.

Fragile Rights/Frederick Bobor James

ACT FIVE SCENE, Seven.

Home of the Kortumas.

Njabu (*Rushes into the parlour from the Jimuis, and meets Tom reading a newspaper.*) You have had the baby boy you have been yearning for. And secondly, you are going to have a puppet of a wife, the type spineless men like you want.

Tom (*Follows Njabu who is heading for the bedroom.*) What are you talking about?

Njabu You will be a stupid fool not to know what I am talking about.

Tom Call me stupid, because I don't know what you are talking about.

Njabu When I am gone, you will understand. (*Drags her suitcase into the parlour.*)

Tom (*Blocks Njabu and there is a scuffle.*) You are going nowhere.

Njabu Get out of my way, Tom. I cannot live in this hell anymore. (*The children come out of their room running.*)

Baindu Mummy, where are you going?

Fragile Rights/Frederick Bobor James

Njabu (*Weeping.*) No definite place, but I am moving out. Your father has got a new wife. Gbessay is your new mother. (*Children try to stop their mother but she runs out of the parlour dragging her suitcase and crying.*)

Light Goes Out.

Fragile Rights/Frederick Bobor James

ACT FIVE, Scene Eight.

At Abie's Residence.

Abie   (*Both Abie and Fasia are drinking beer.*) You are not serious about deserting your wife, are you?

Fasia   I am a fool to run to you each time I have a problem with my wife.

Abie   Just as I am a fool to think that you can bring happiness here, after you have wounded the heart of another woman. (*Njabu comes dragging a suitcase.*) Why do you come dragging a suitcase?

Njabu   (*In tears.*) Tom has broken my heart.

Abie   (*Anxious.*) What has he done?

Njabu   He is the father of our maid's two-day-old baby. Tom has been doing all sorts of evil things to me, but this is the last straw. (*She weeps, and Abie begins to cry with her.*)

Fasia   Marriage is a forest. Seen from a distance, it is even and beautiful from the outside. But when you enter it, in spite of fruits, flowers, and other beautiful attractions you may find there, you are bound to find thorns, scorepions, snakes, lions and what else? (*Tom enters with the children.*) Genies, yes genies. It is a mixture of sweetness and bitterness. We do not need to be at odds with each other to be equals. It is better to pursue gender equality in partnership. With planning, love, respect and responsibility, we can achieve what our women want, with time. Militant drumming of it in the ears will not go far. I am going back to my wife. From now on, I will listen to her, and try hard to please her. I will adjust so that we can move forward, in peace.

Abie Well, it looks like I have to mend fences with my husband. Fasia, you were right when you said that a person that preaches change should set examples for others to follow. I now realize that I cannot change my husband when I am away from him. It takes a lot of patience, reasoning and tact to teach old dog new tricks.

Tom Njabu, please accept my apology for all the physical attacks and the excessive drinking I indulged in. (*The children look at their parents, beaming with smiles.*)

Njabu I owe you and the children an apology too, Tom. I became obsessed with WLM to the

	extent that I neglected the welfare of my children and the unity and peace of my home.
Tom	Now that we understand where we were both going wrong, we can bring things back to normal. The world is always changing, and I am a part of the changing world. I will give you all the support needed to make WLM move forward. Who knows, one of my daughters may become the first female head of state of this country, and that will not happen without an institution such as the WLM.
Njabu	*(Looking at Tom in his eyes.)* Gbessay has a future, too. We have to send her to a vocational institution, and support her child.
Tom	We will discuss that at home.

Light Fades.

THE END.

Fragile Rights/Frederick Bobor James

GLOSSARY OF LOCAL WORDS

1. **Sande** Also known as Bundu/Bundo/Bondo, is a female secret society mostly in West African counries, where female genital mutilation/cutting (FGM/C) is practised.

2. **Poro** A secret society in Sierra Leone that is responsible for organizing the initiation of boys and young men for adult life.

3. **Togbehs** These are boys/young men who join Poro society at the same time--Poromates.

4. **Massah** A corrupted form of the word Master.

5. **Missisi** A corrupted form of of the word Missus.

6. **Kwo-o-o** An exclamation in Mende.

7. **Mende** The language spoken by the Mende ethnic group in Sierra Leone.

8. **Sampa** A half-masked female dancer who is connected with the Sande society. There are also male Sampa dancers.

9. **Tomosi** A corrupted form of the name Thomas, especially by Mende speakers in Sierra Leone.

Fragile Rights/Frederick Bobor James

10. **Cassava leaves**   Cassava leaves, okra, and broad beans are the different kinds of sauce prepared to be eaten with Sierra Leonean foods such as rice, cassava tubers, water yam, etc.

www.ingramcontent.com/pod-product-compliance
Lightning Source LLC
Chambersburg PA
CBHW020005050426
42450CB00005B/315